Welcome all to my lil coffee table photo book. This book is a collection of photographs taken by me in the Walden area in the state of New York. All these photographs were taken with a normal Nikkon camera then reworked in a paint program for the Pastel Painting look.

        I hope you all enjoy the photos.

          More Books To Come...

Feel free to e-mail me at kenscreationslive@yahoo.com

I can also be reached at #(845) 713-4131

I also have from clothing to coffee cups and more

On these following sites,

Vida and Zazzle.

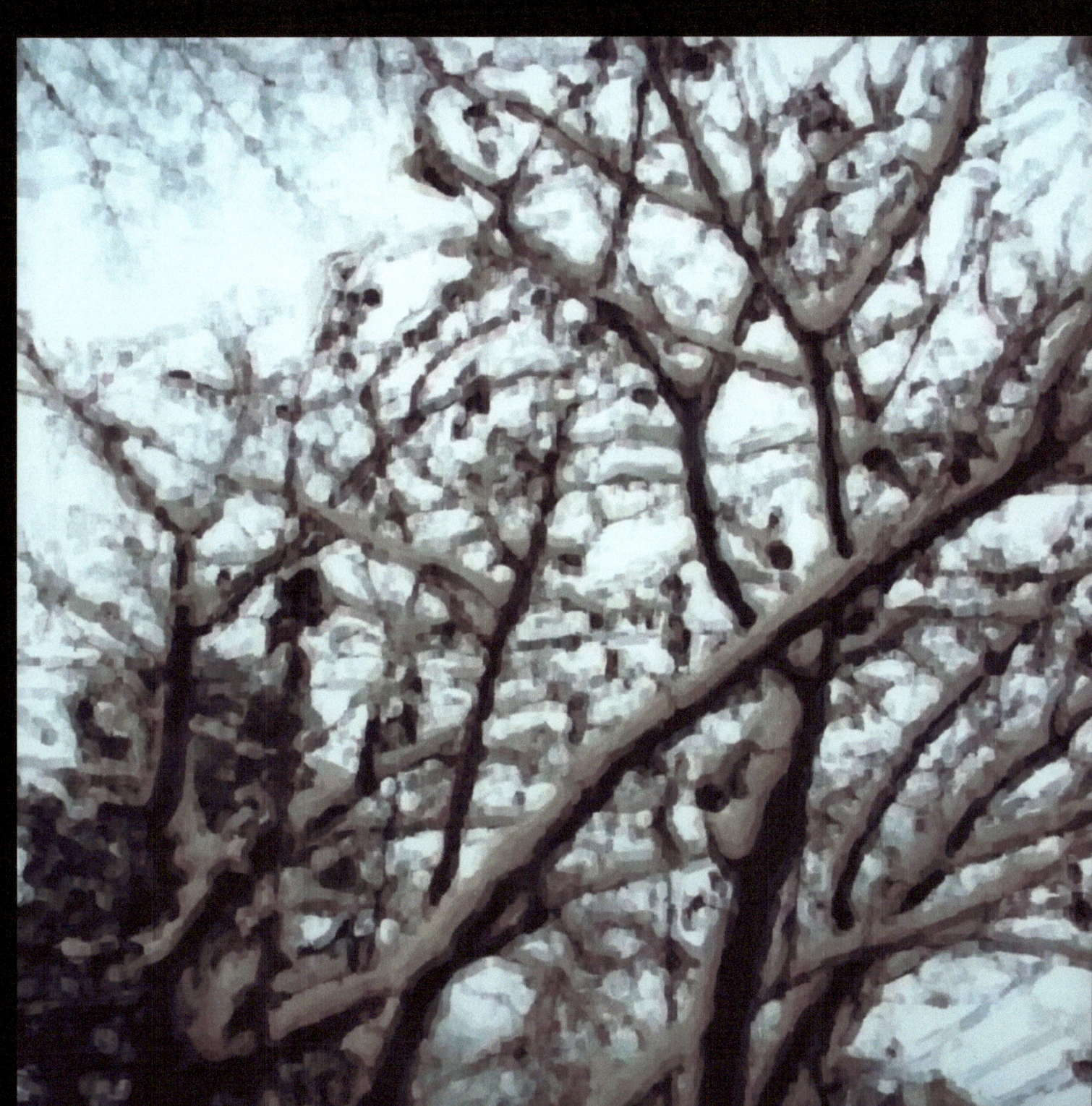

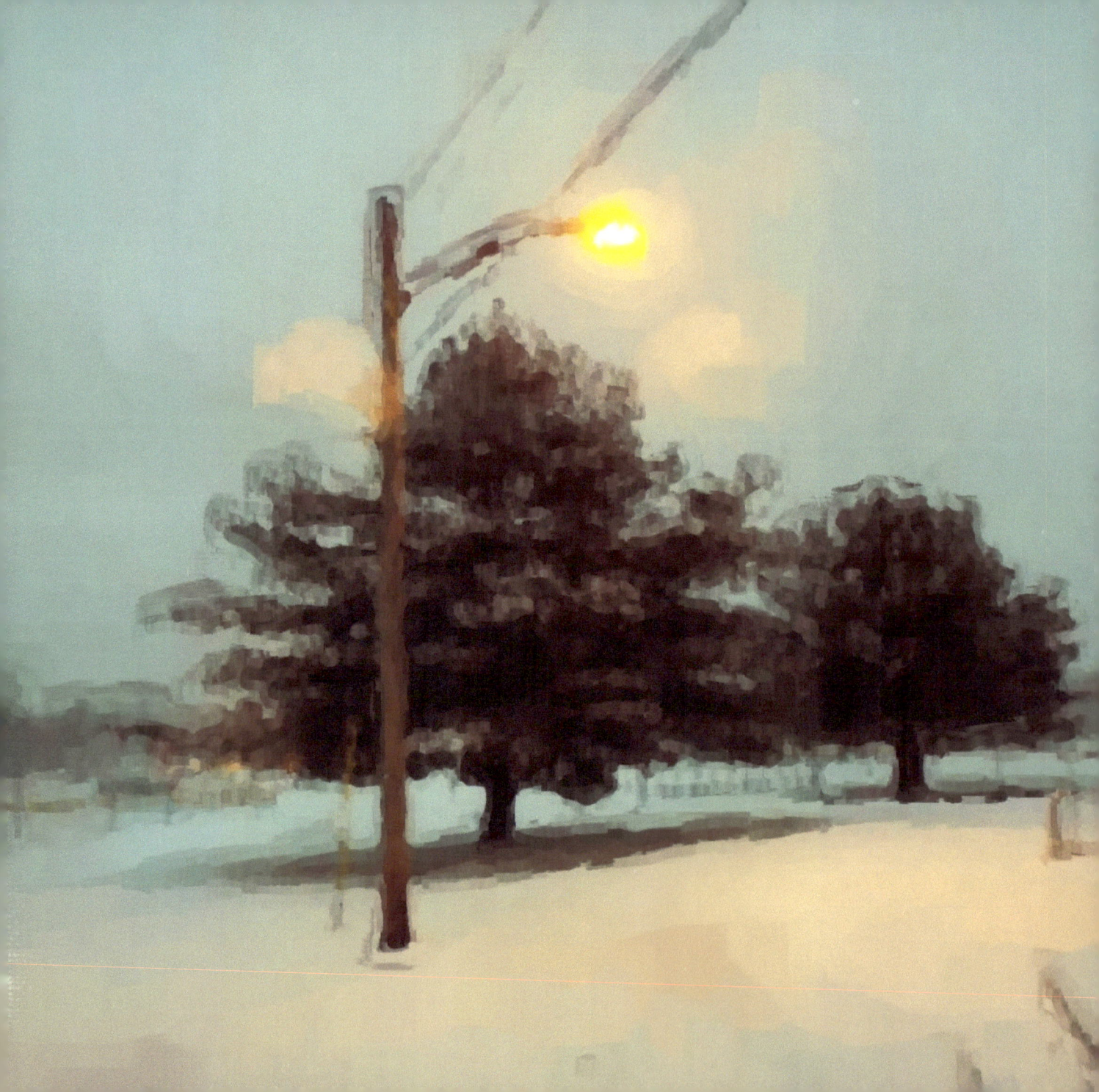

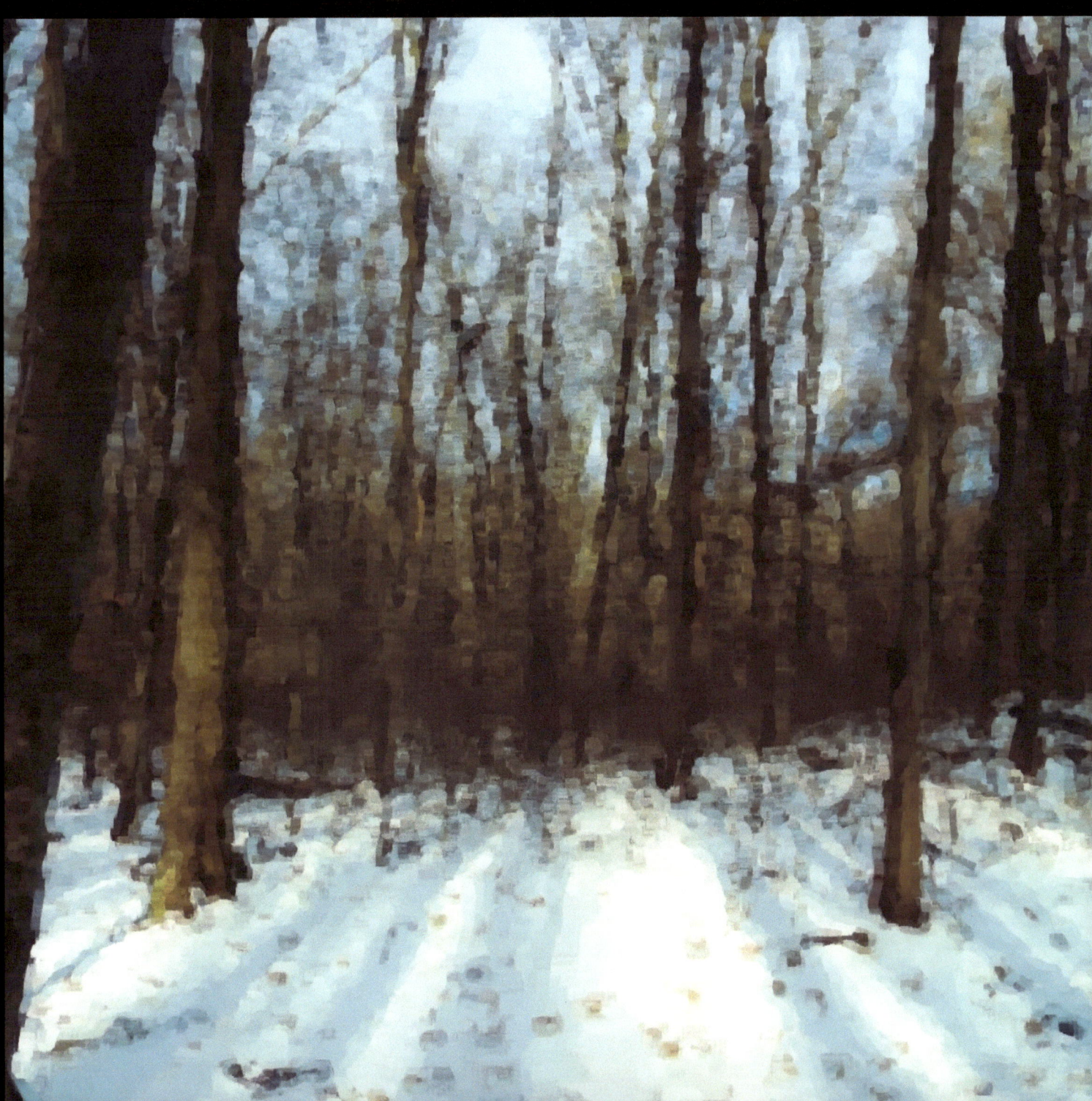

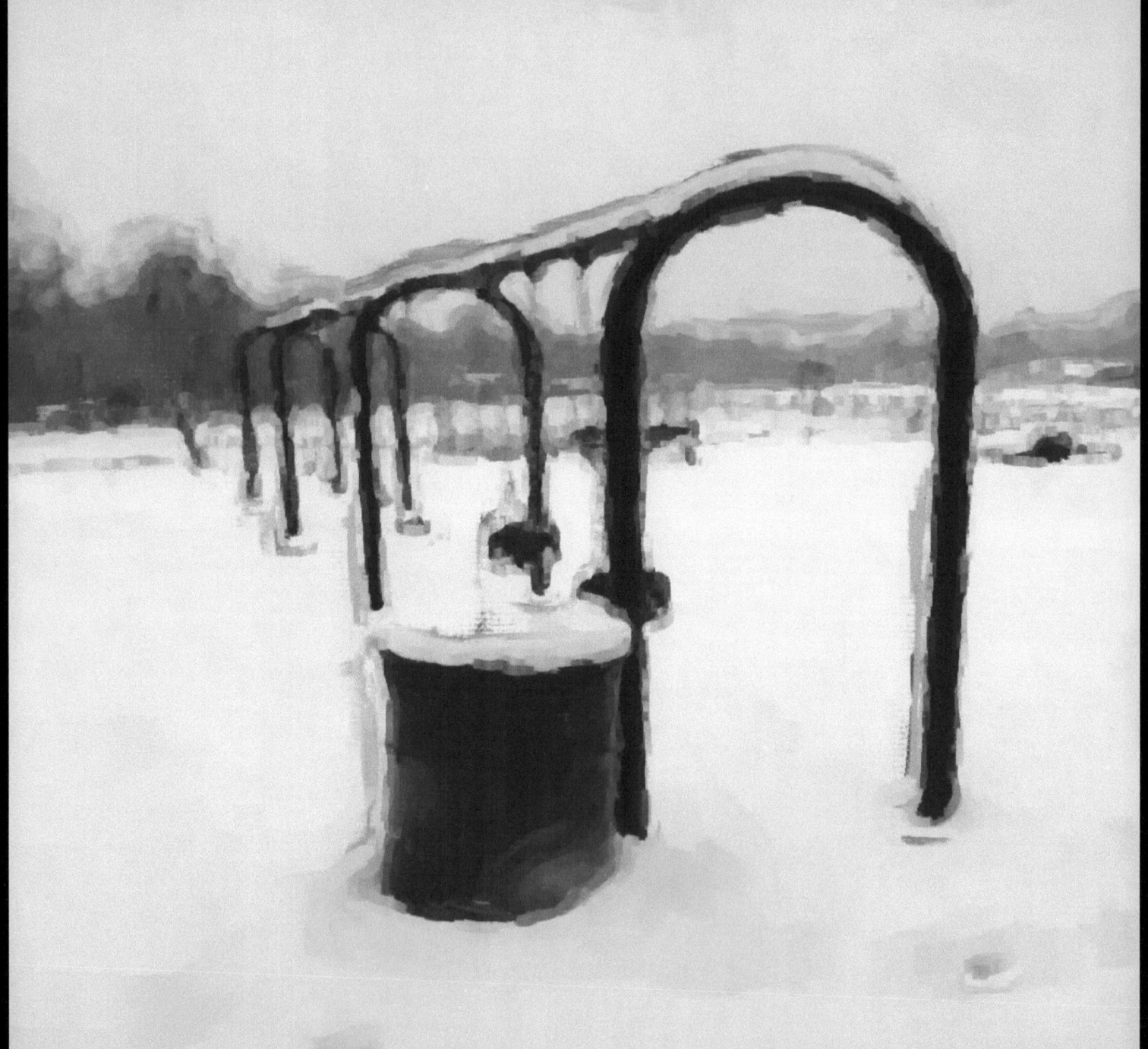

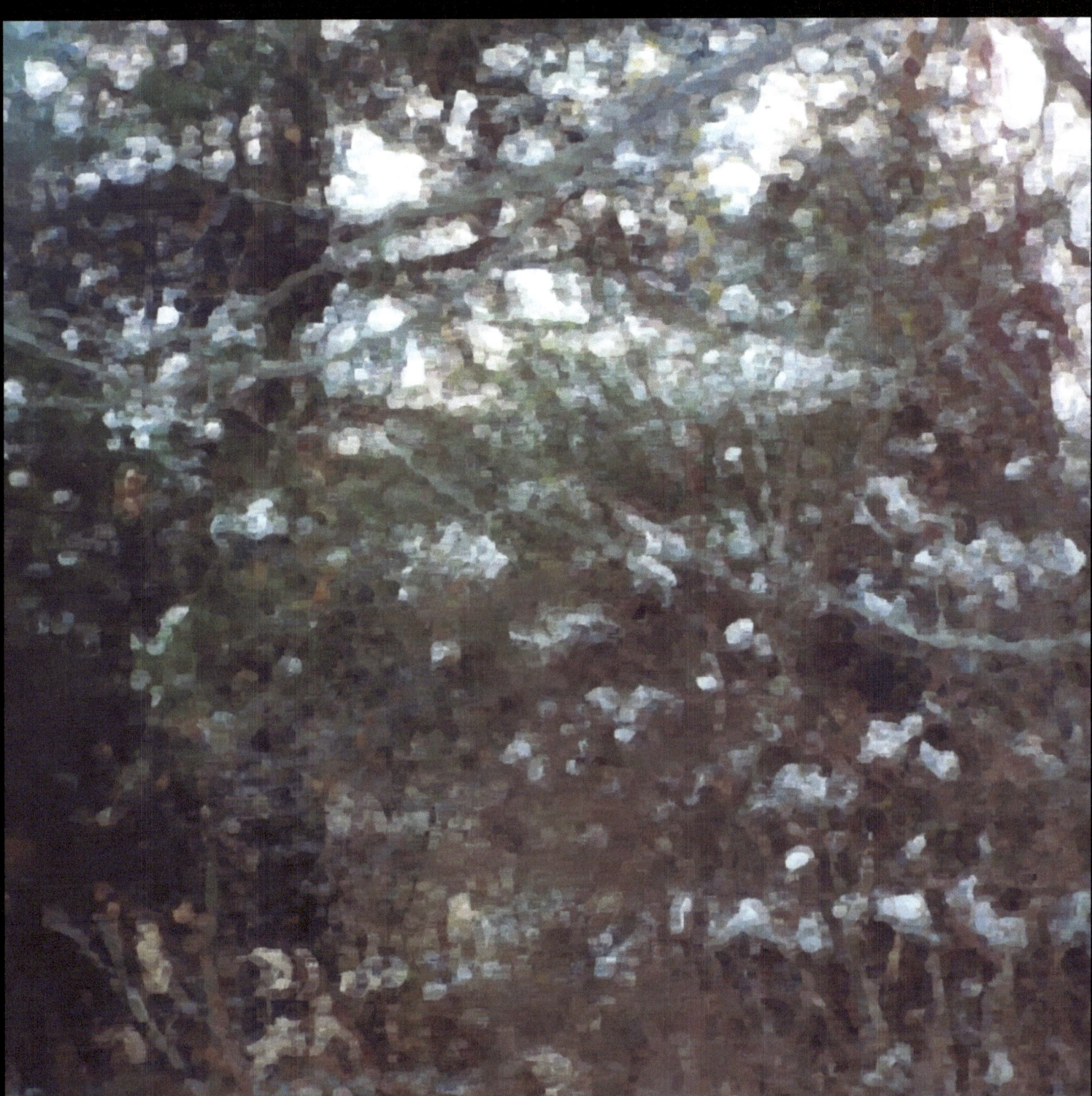

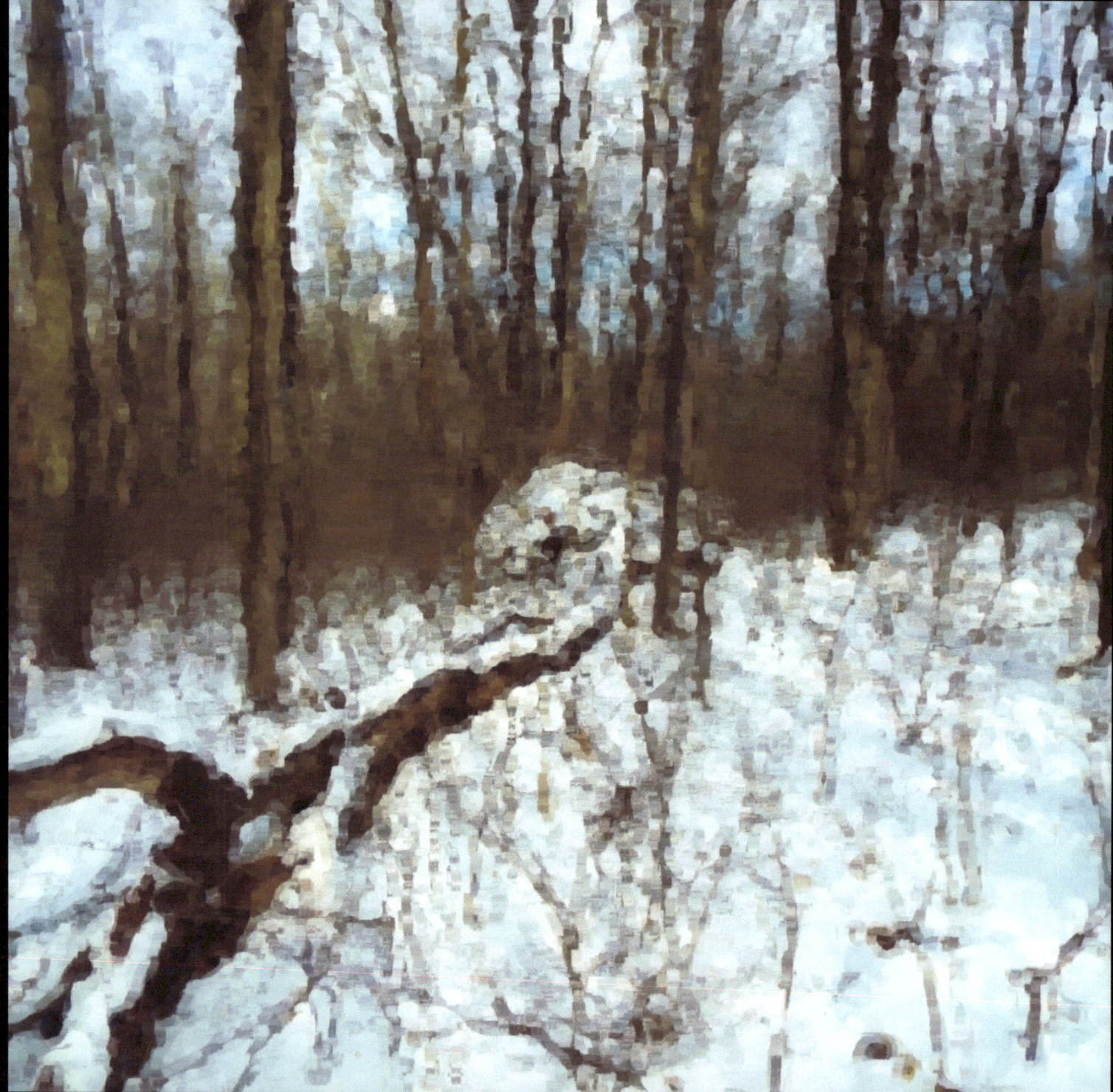

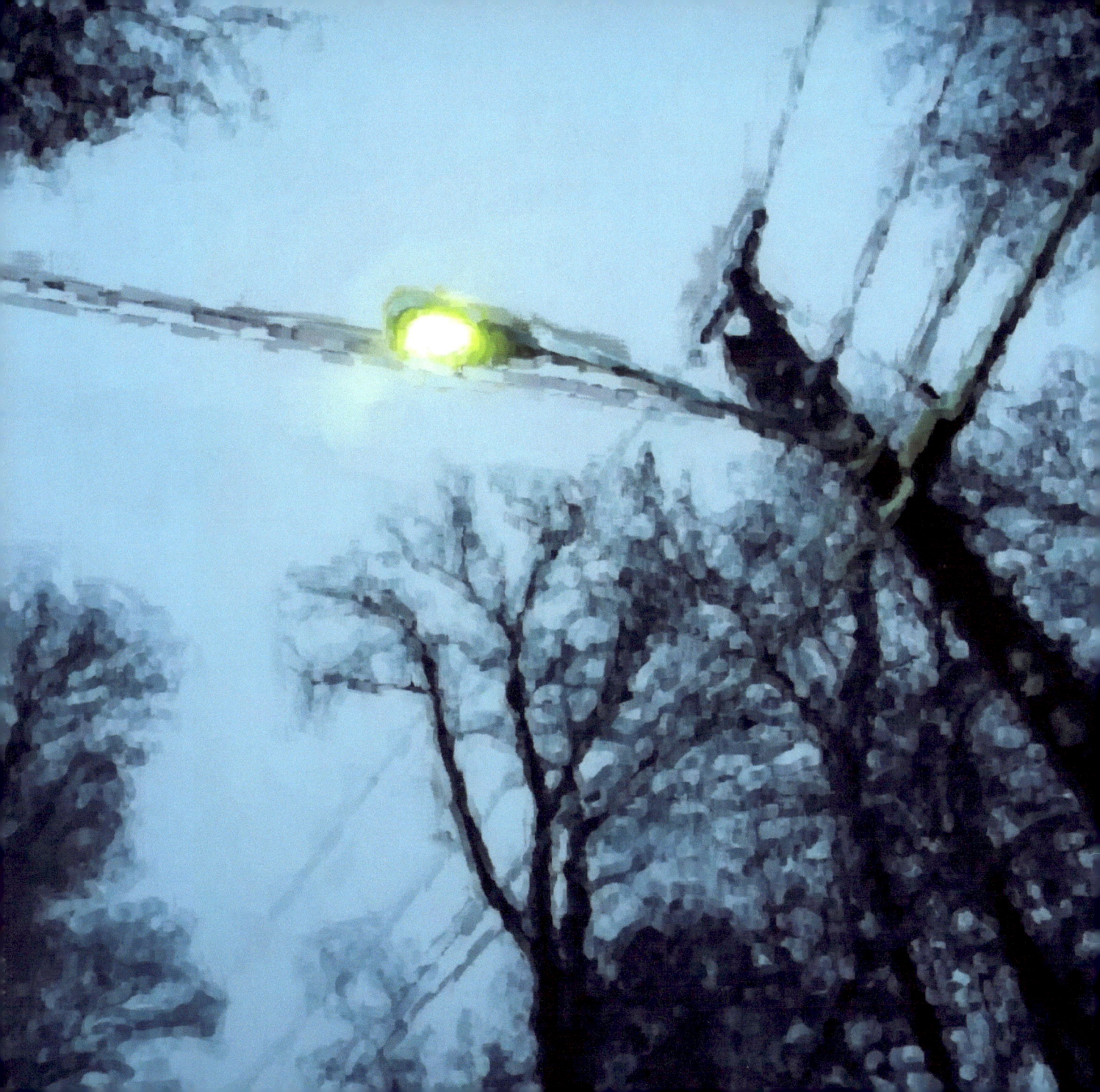

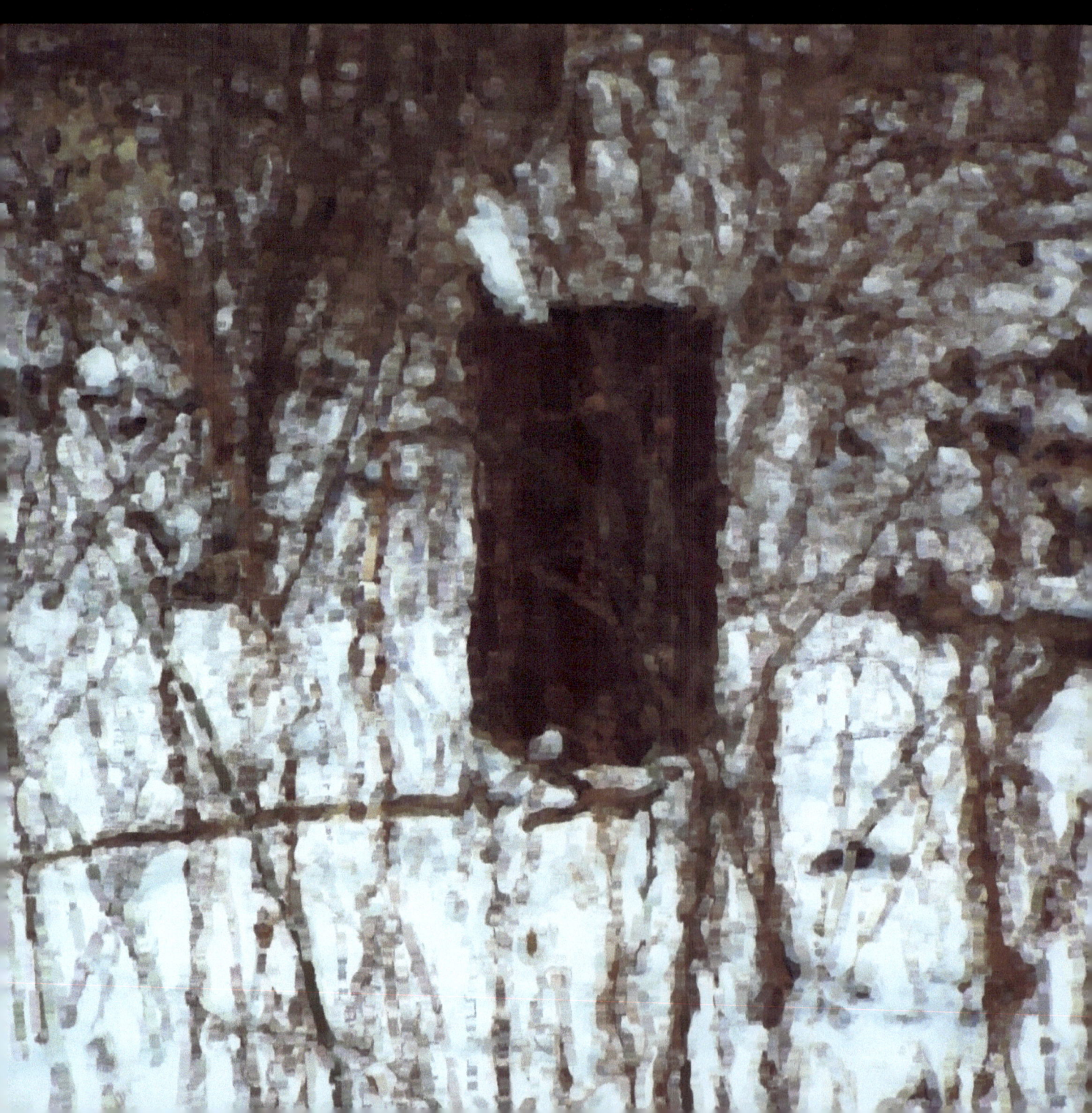

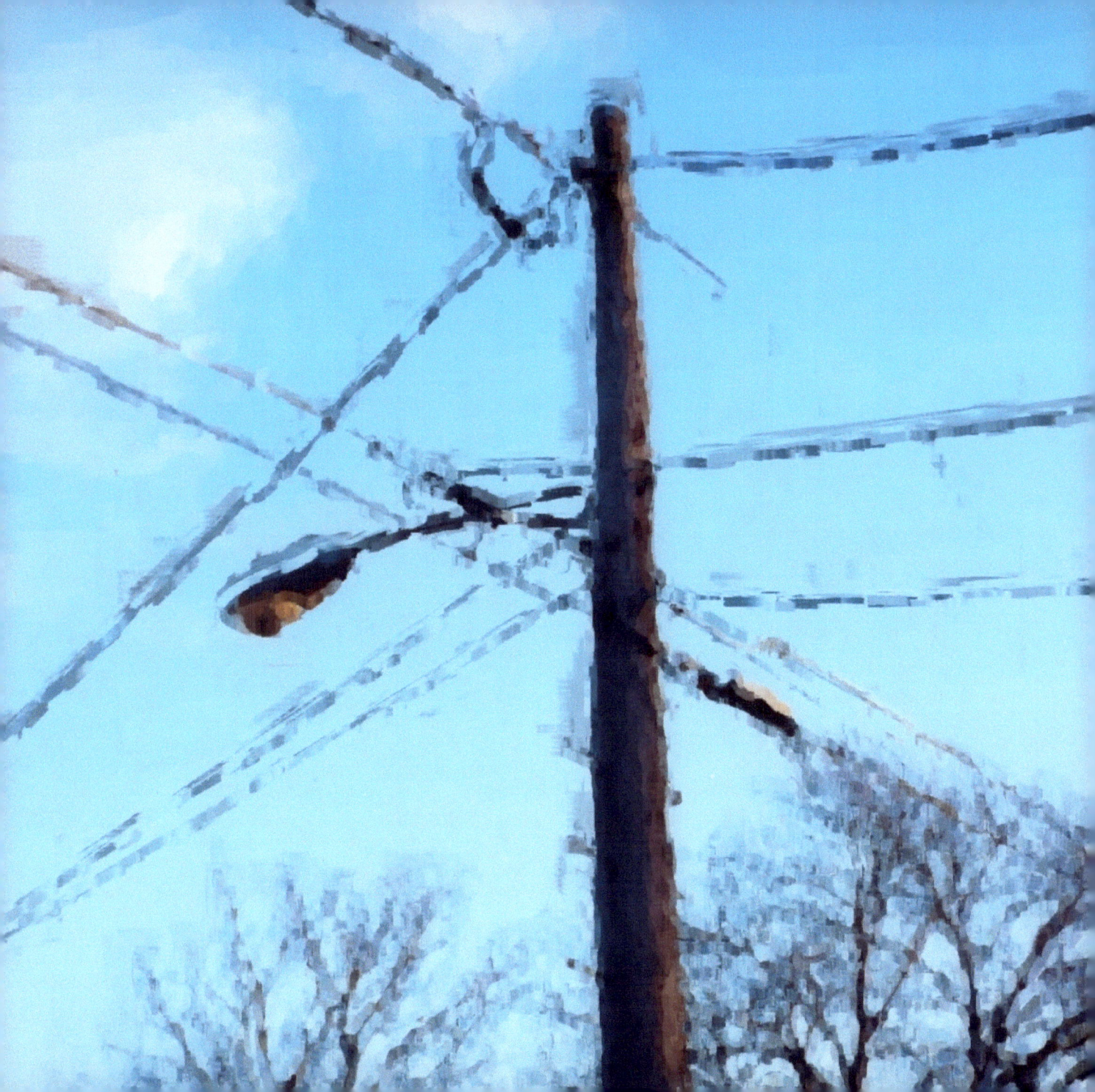

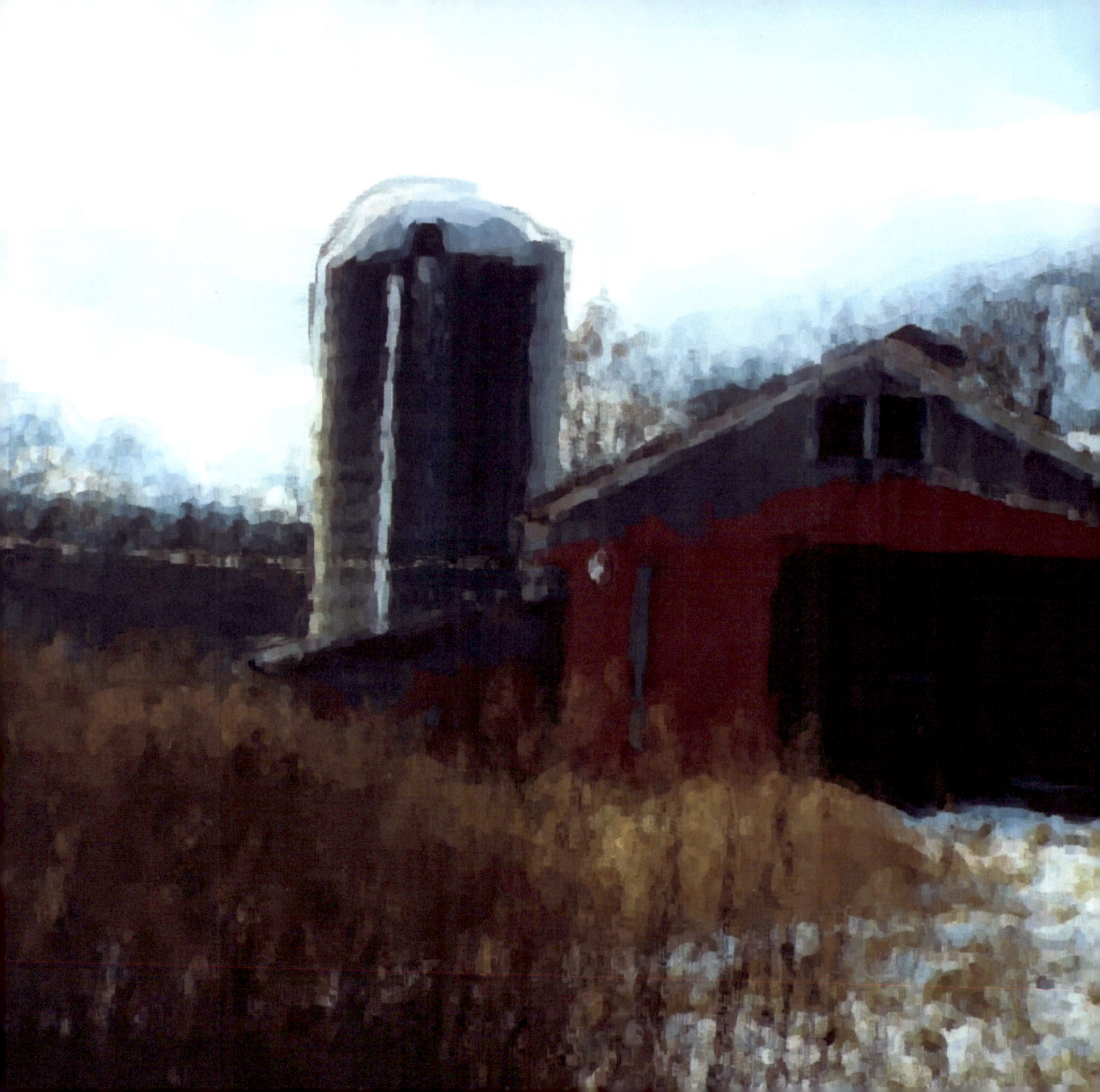

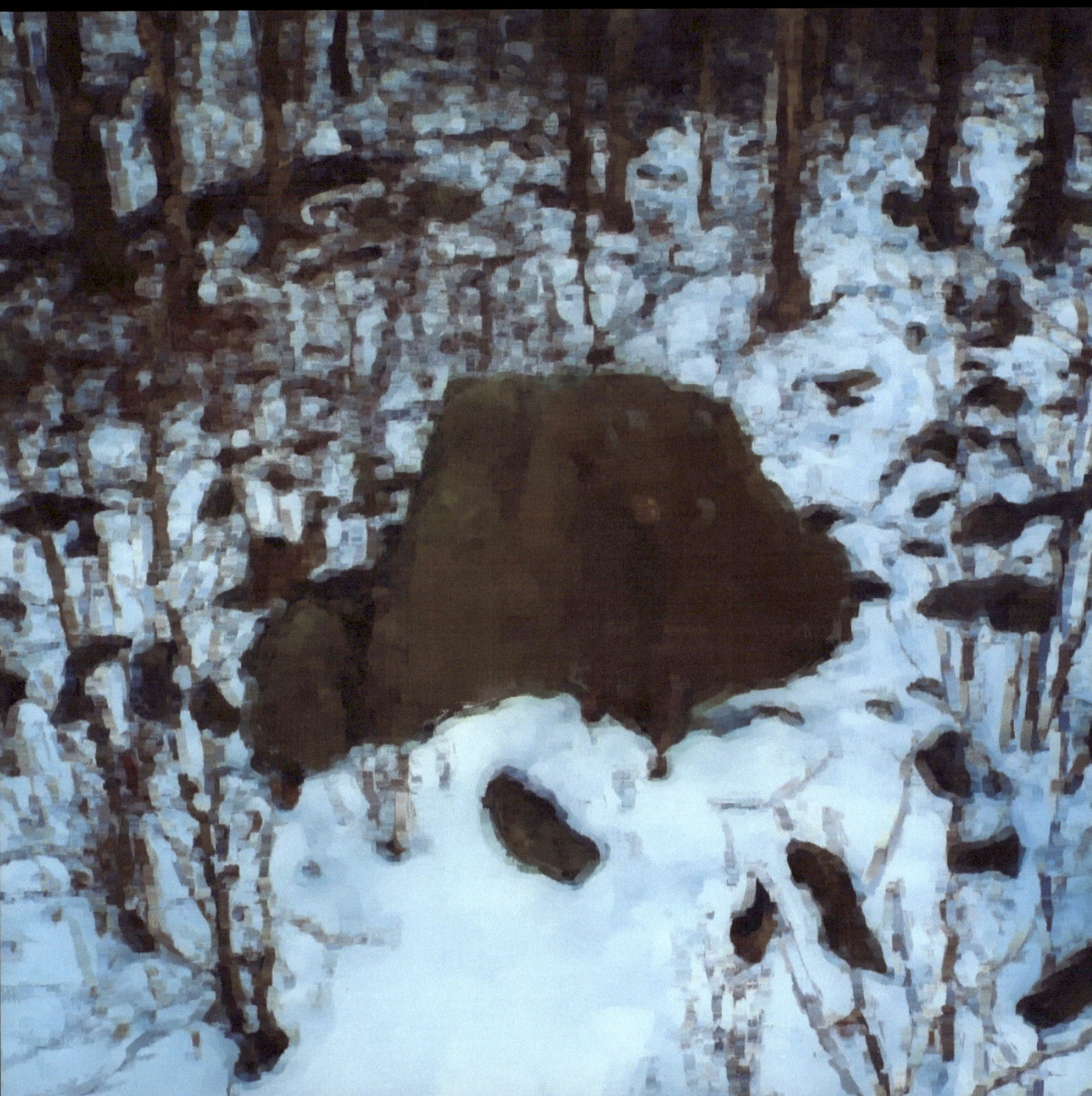

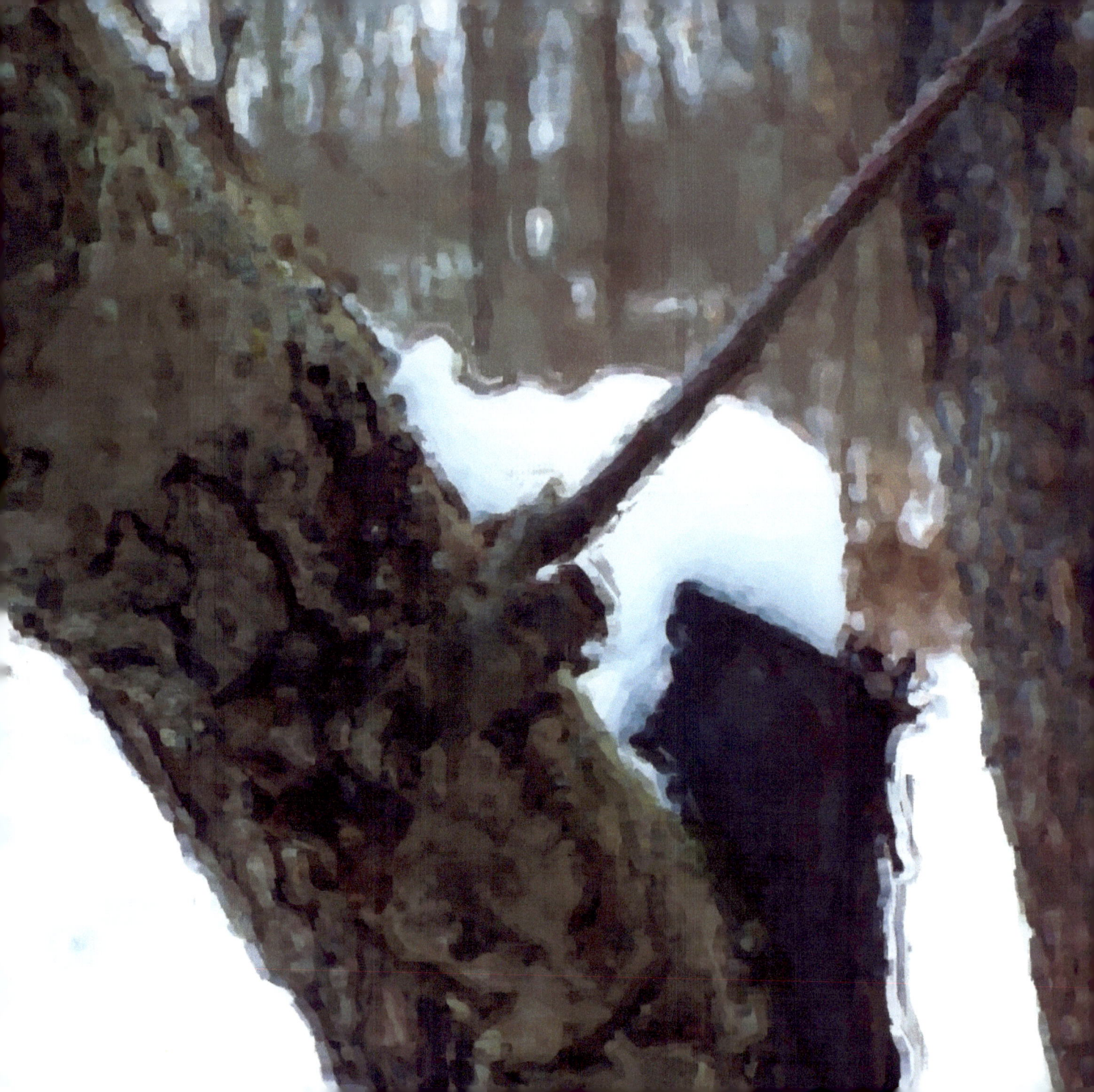

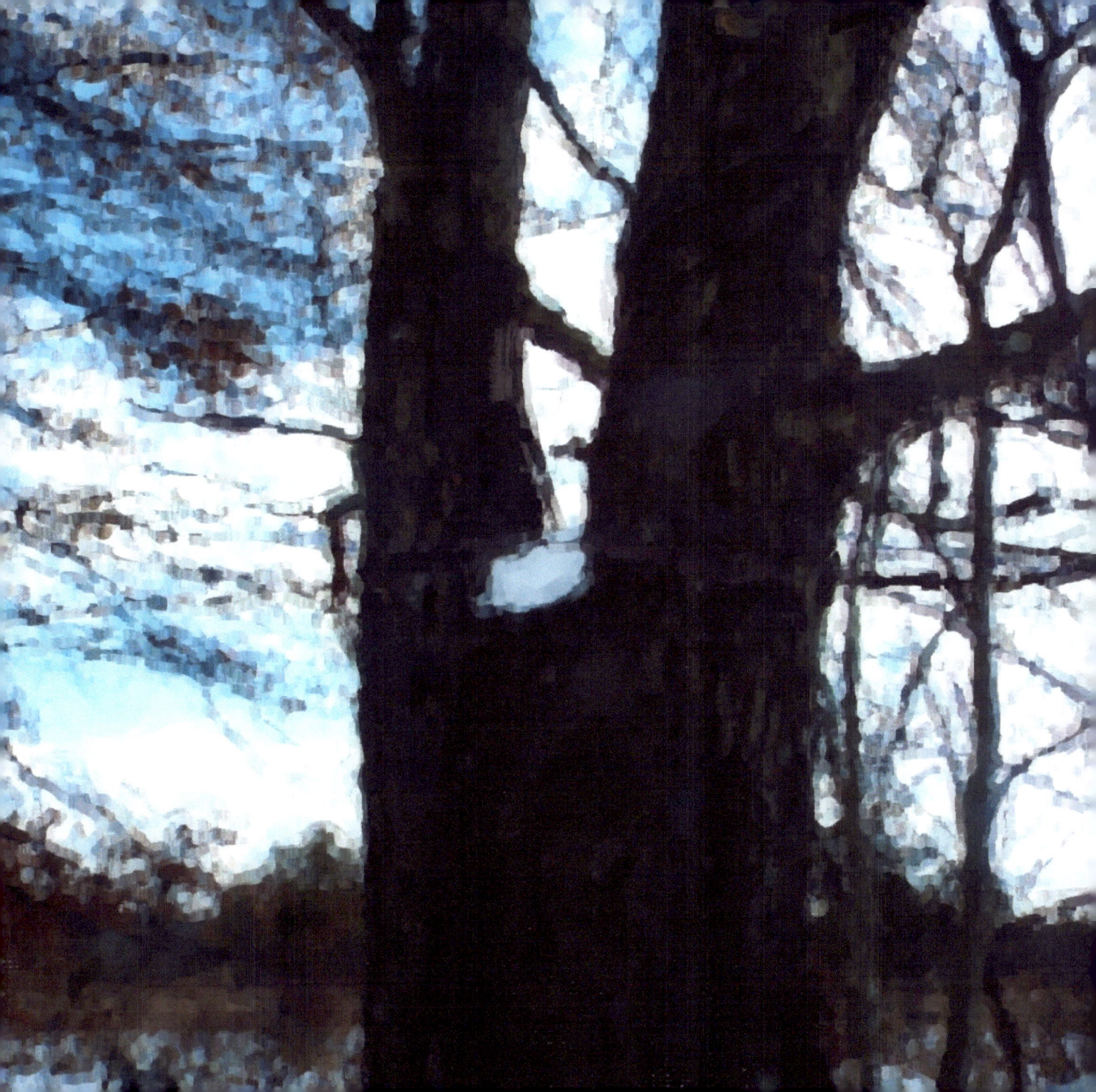

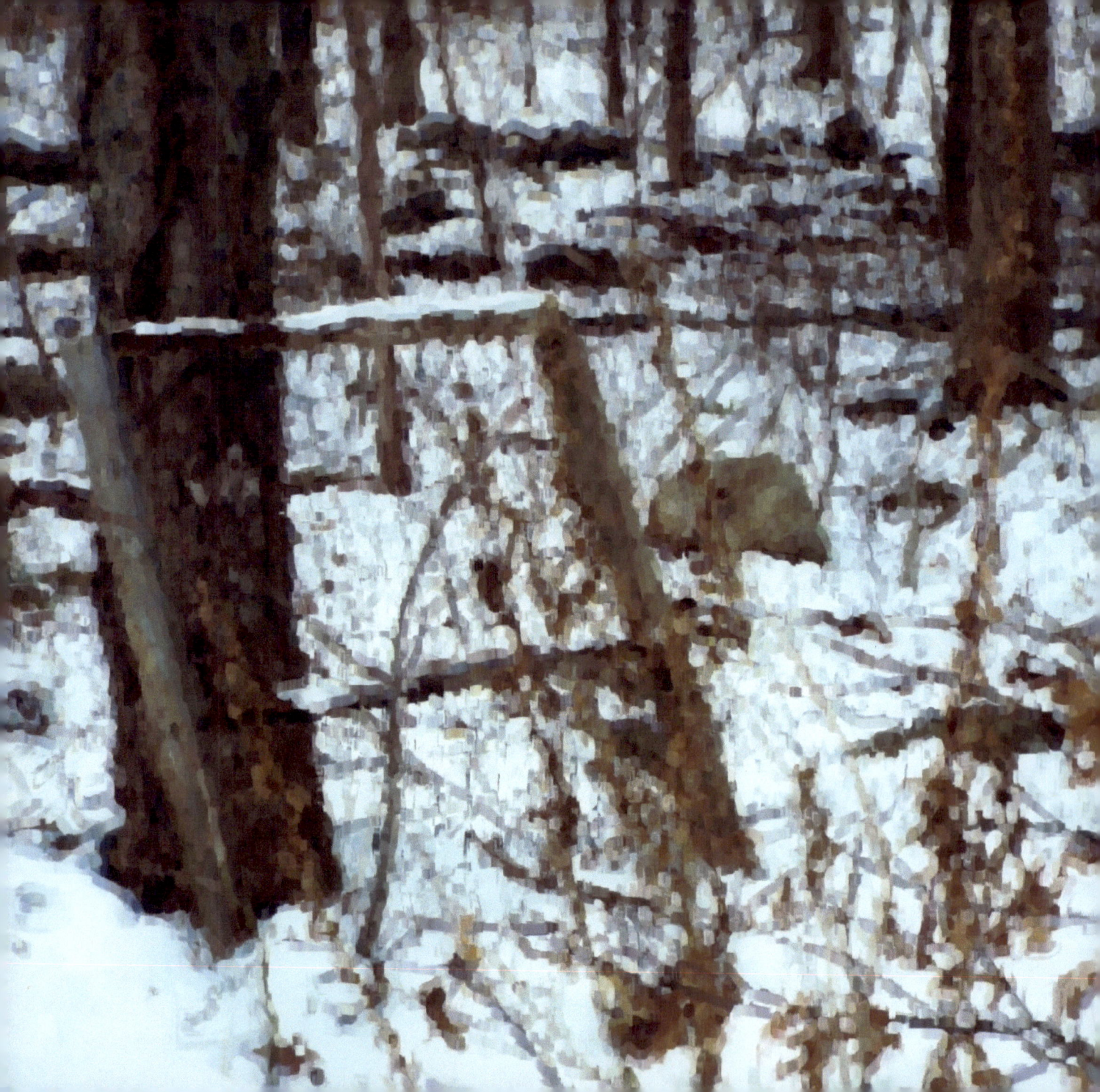

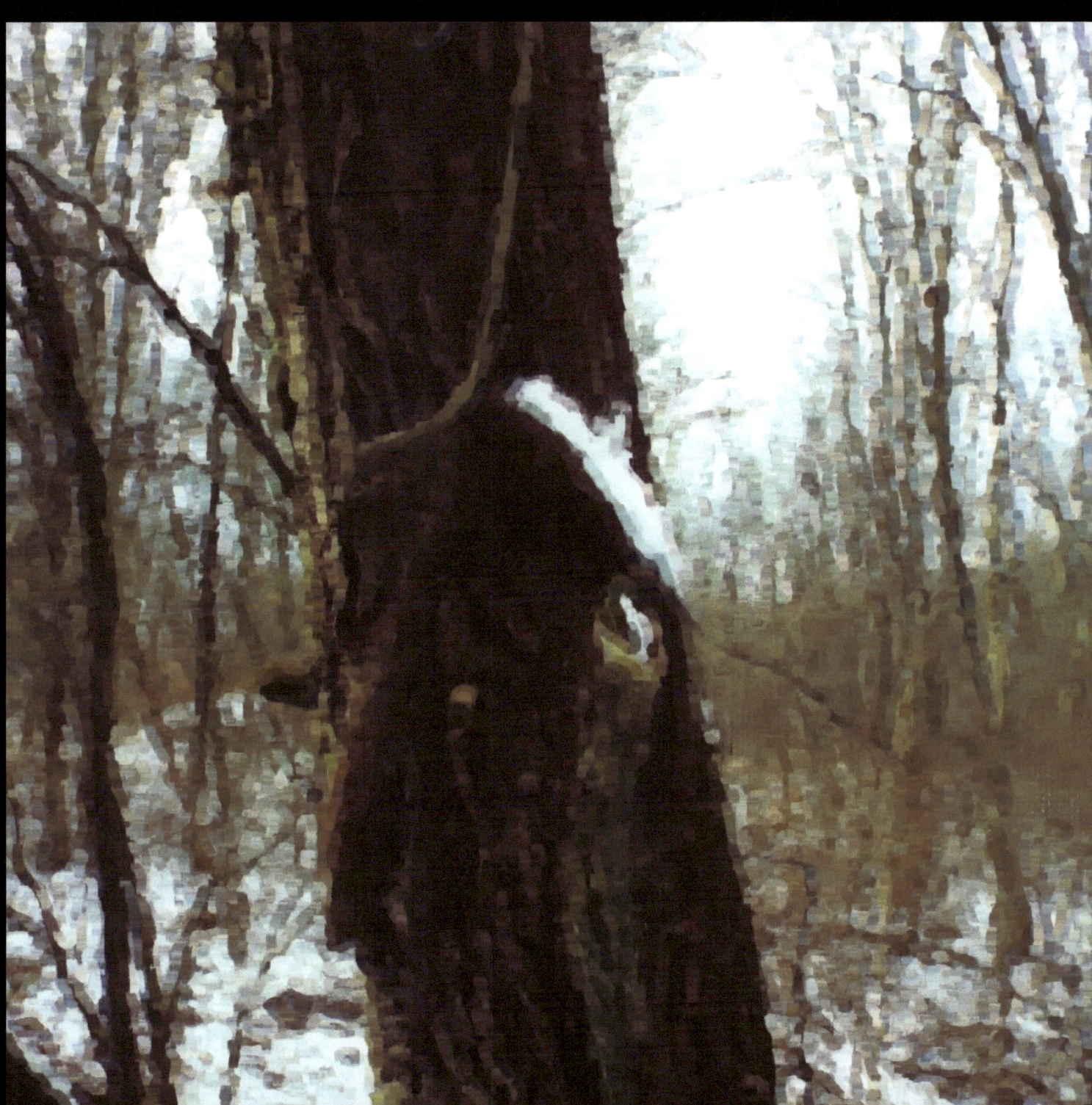

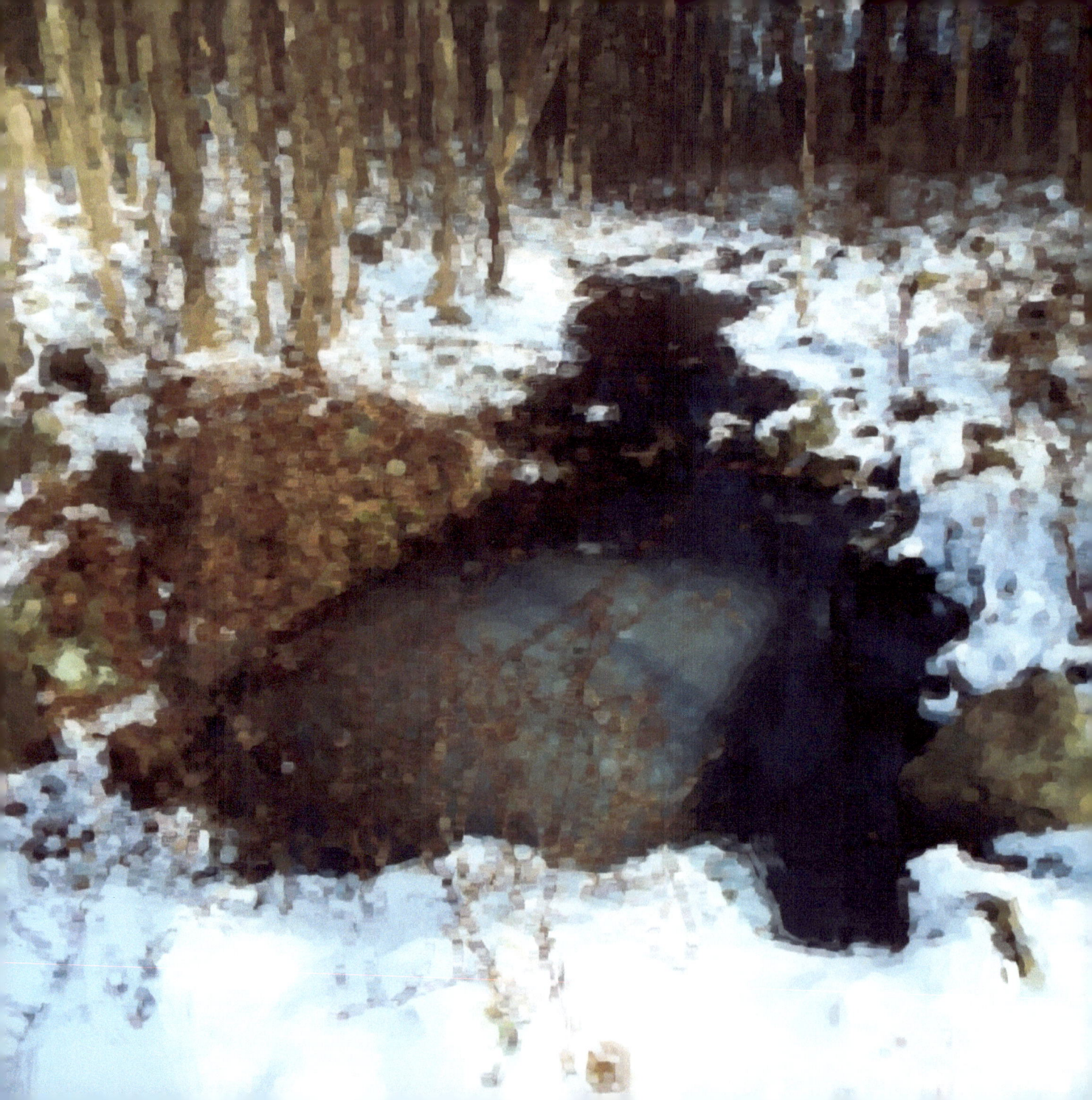

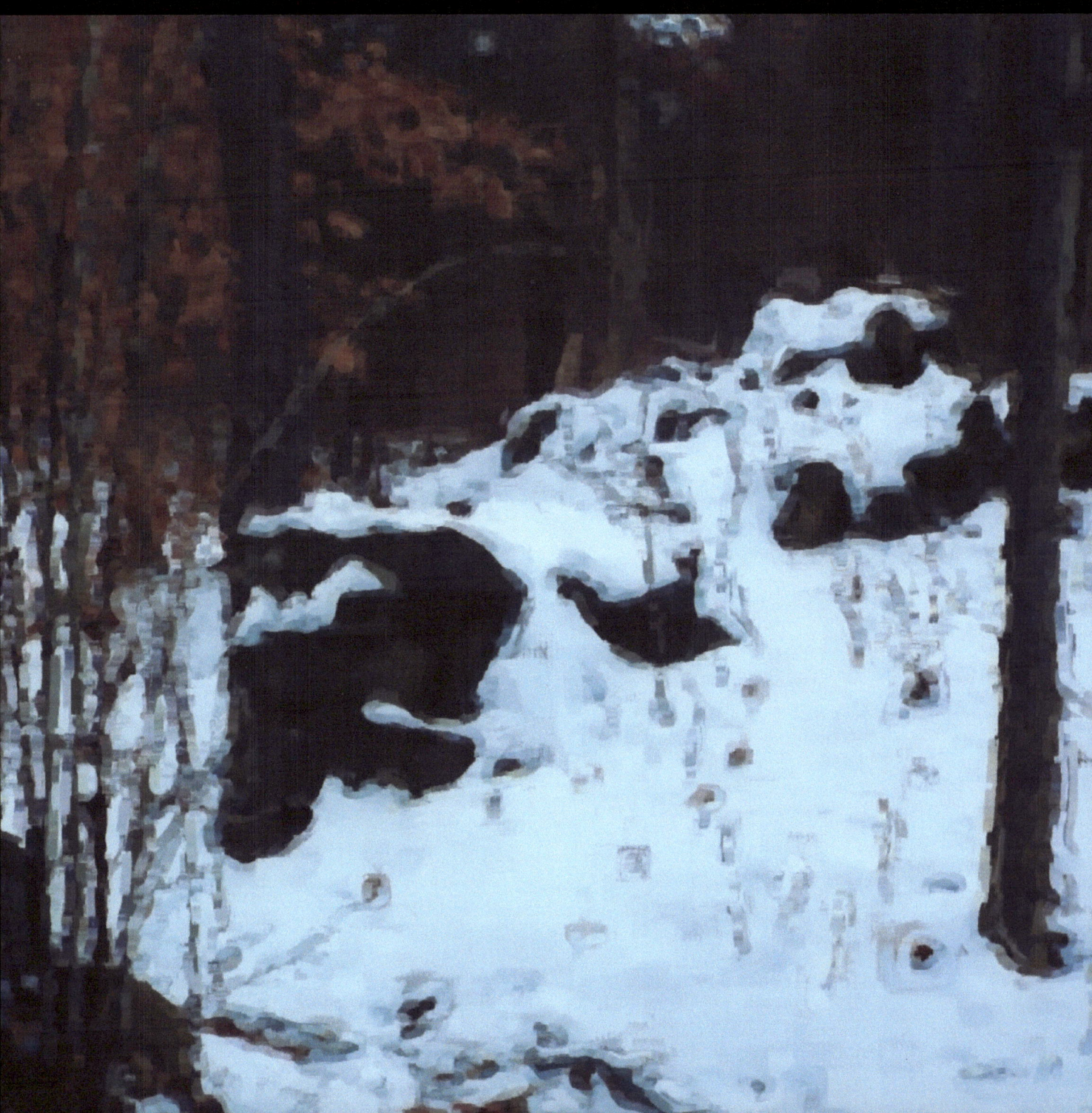

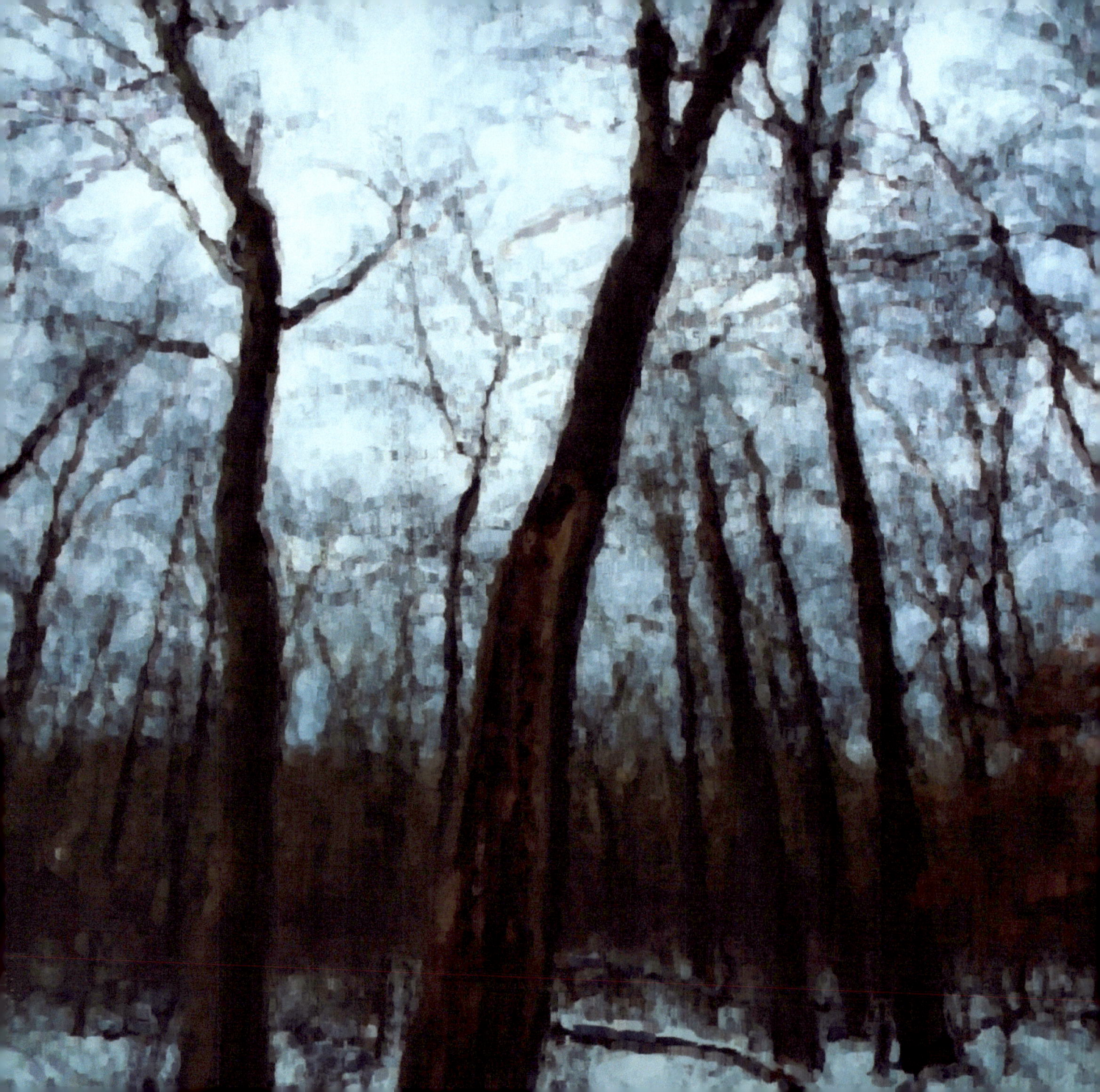

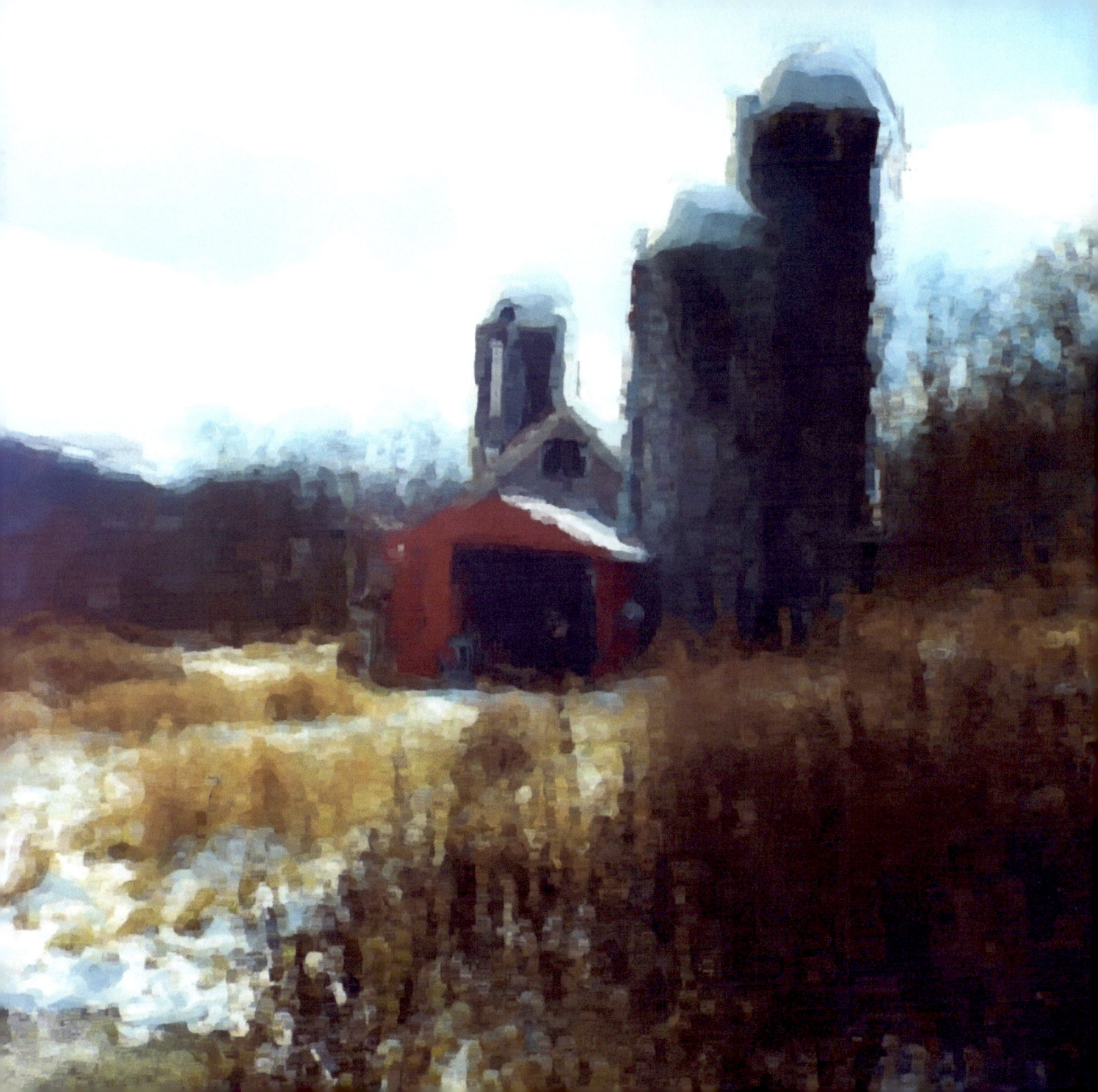

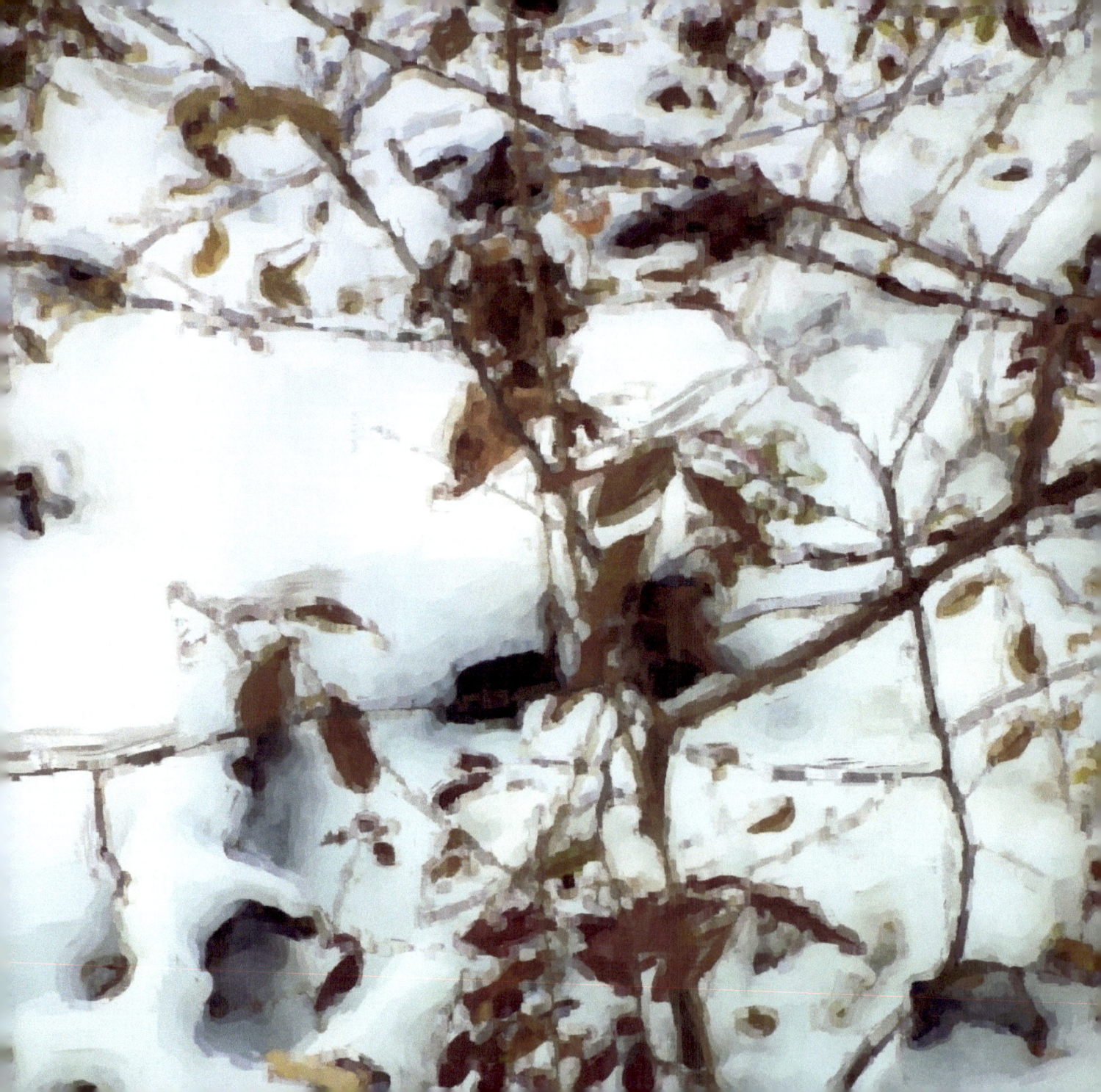

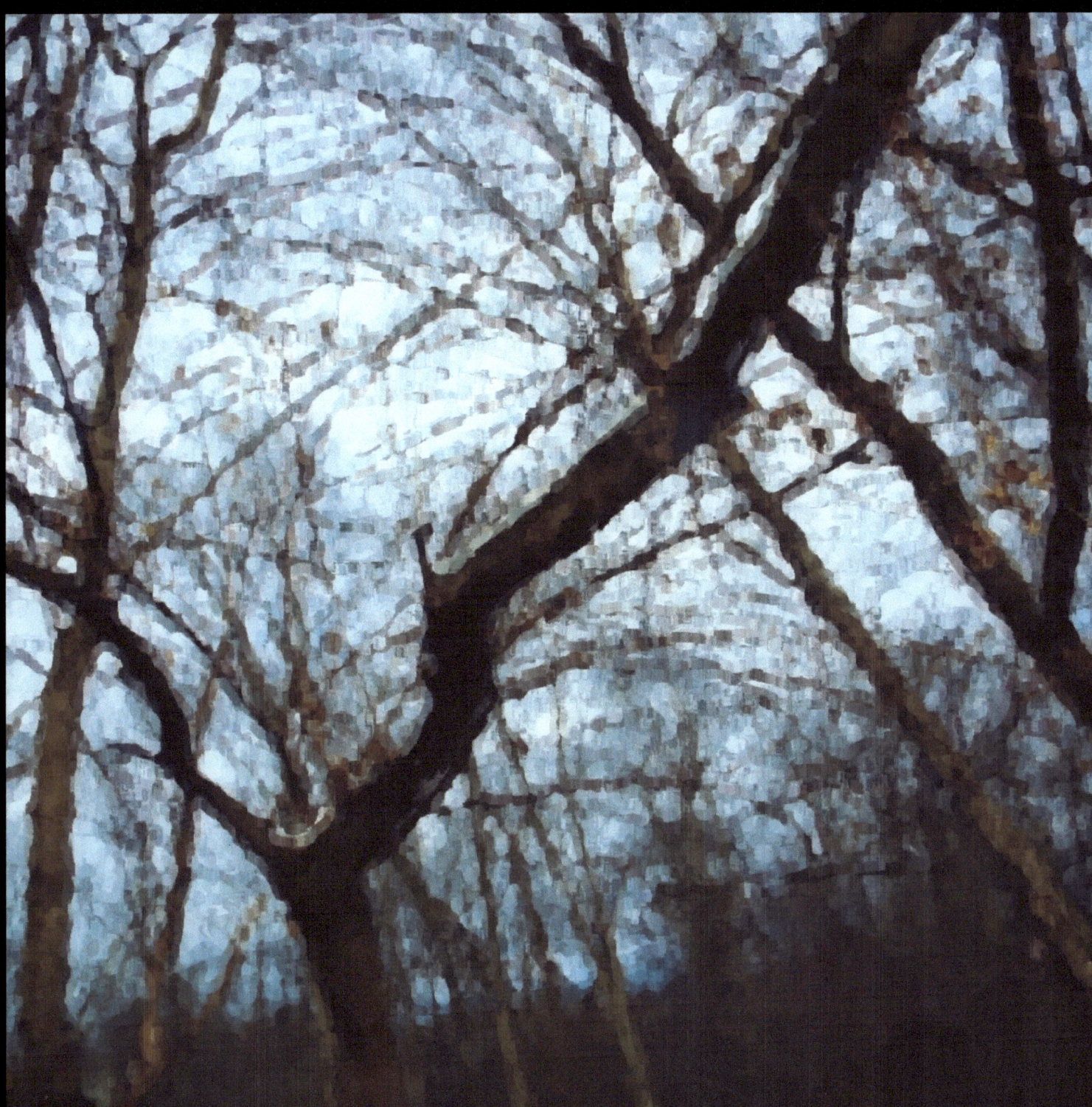

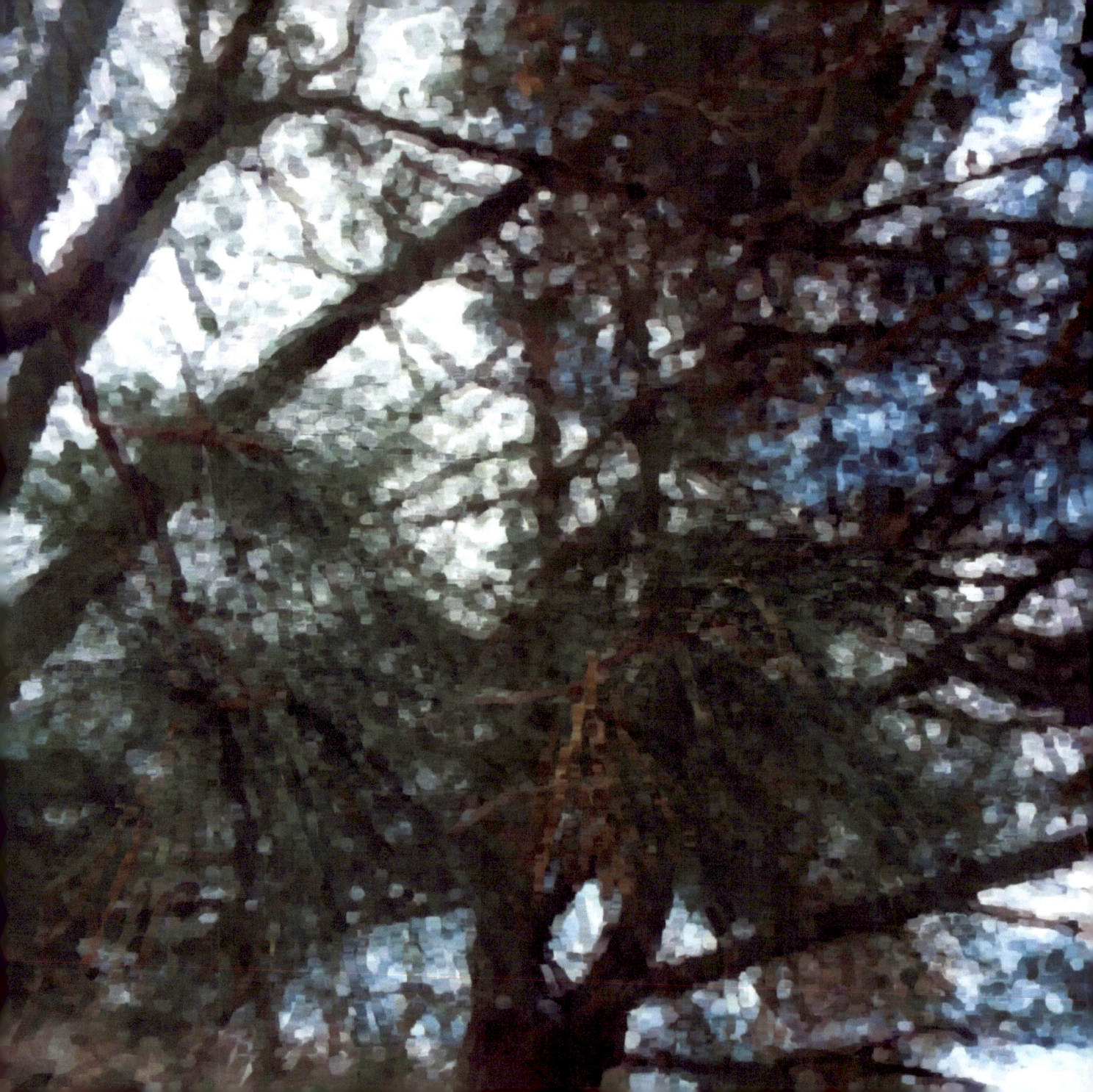

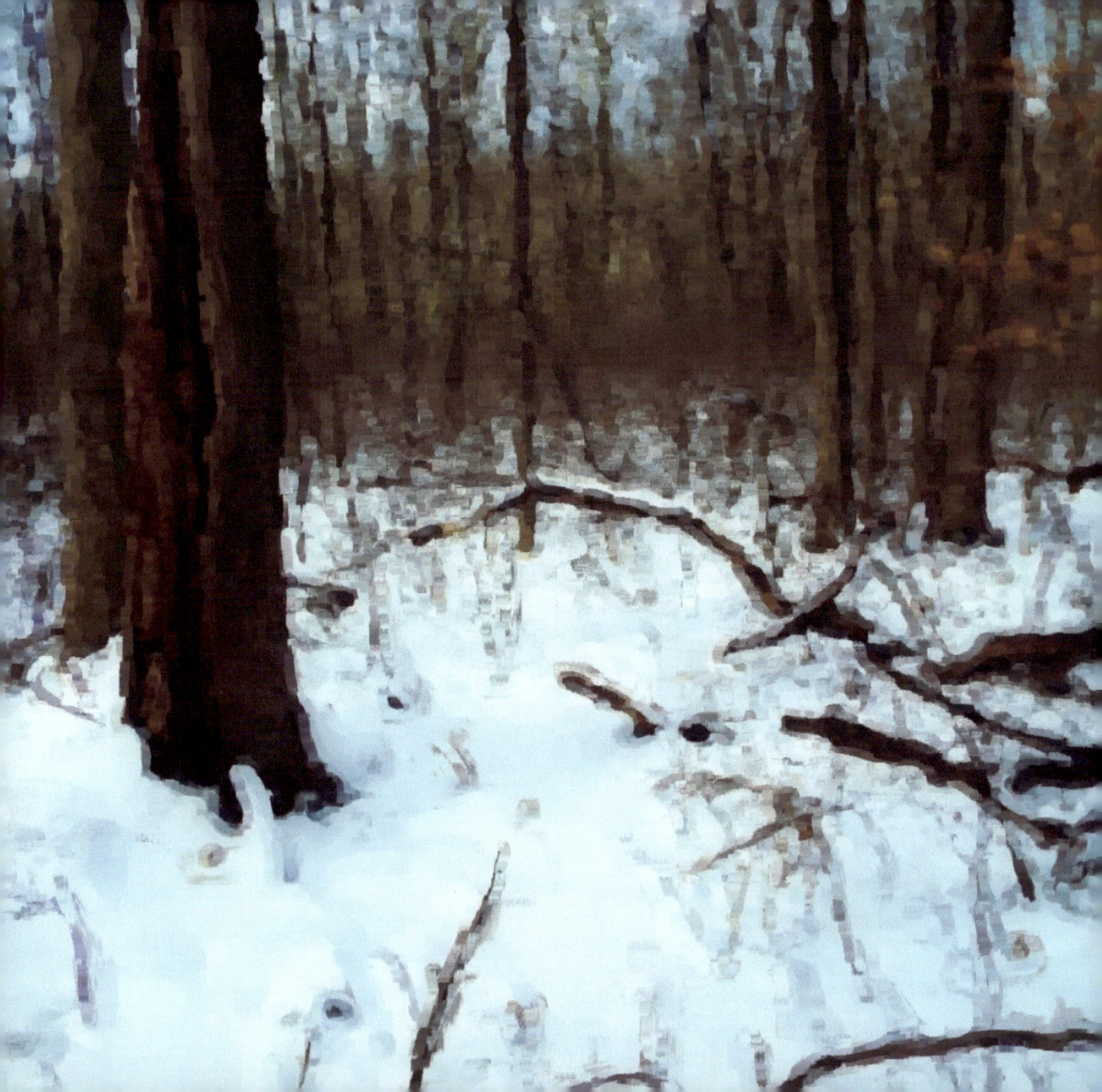

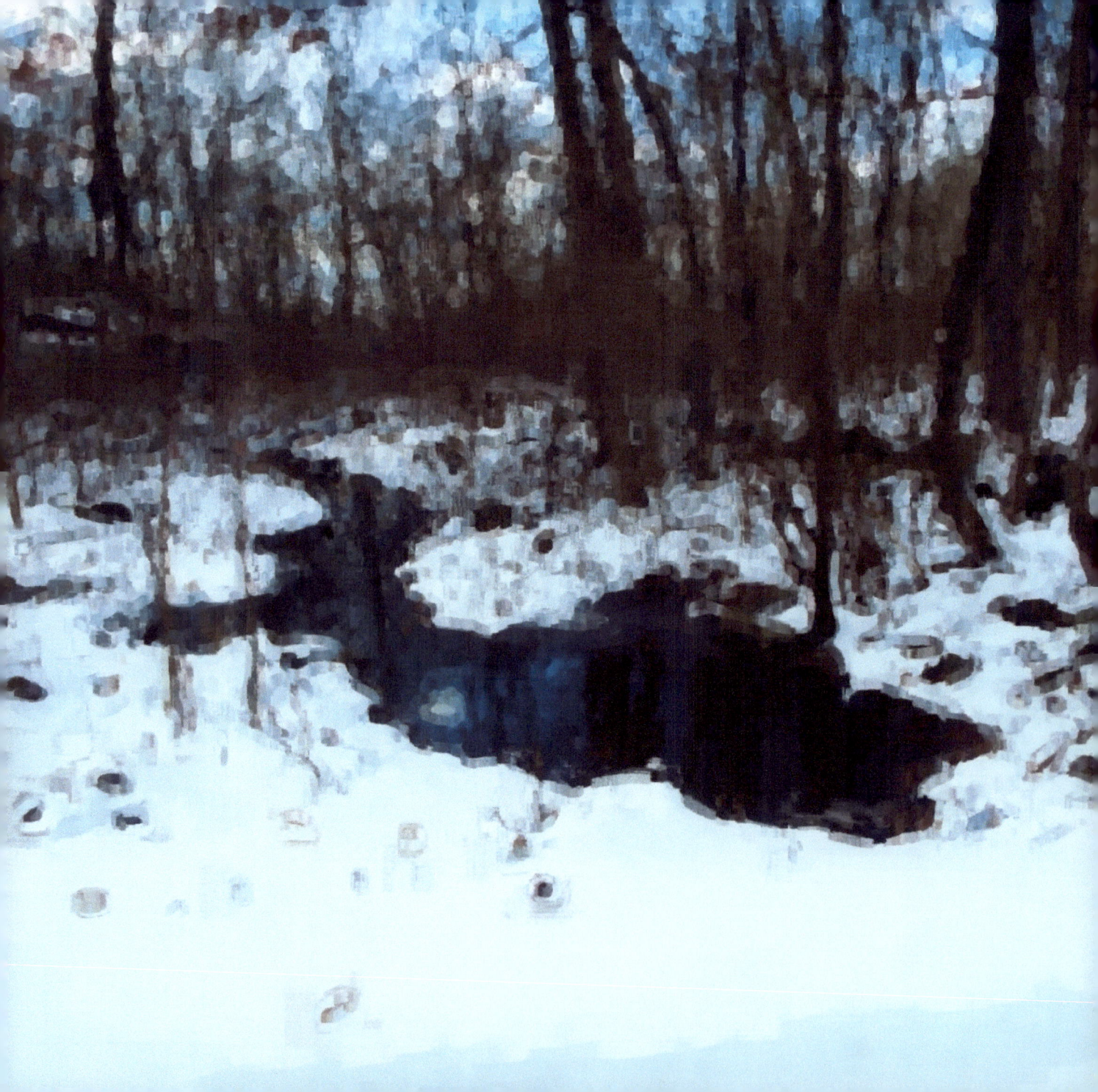

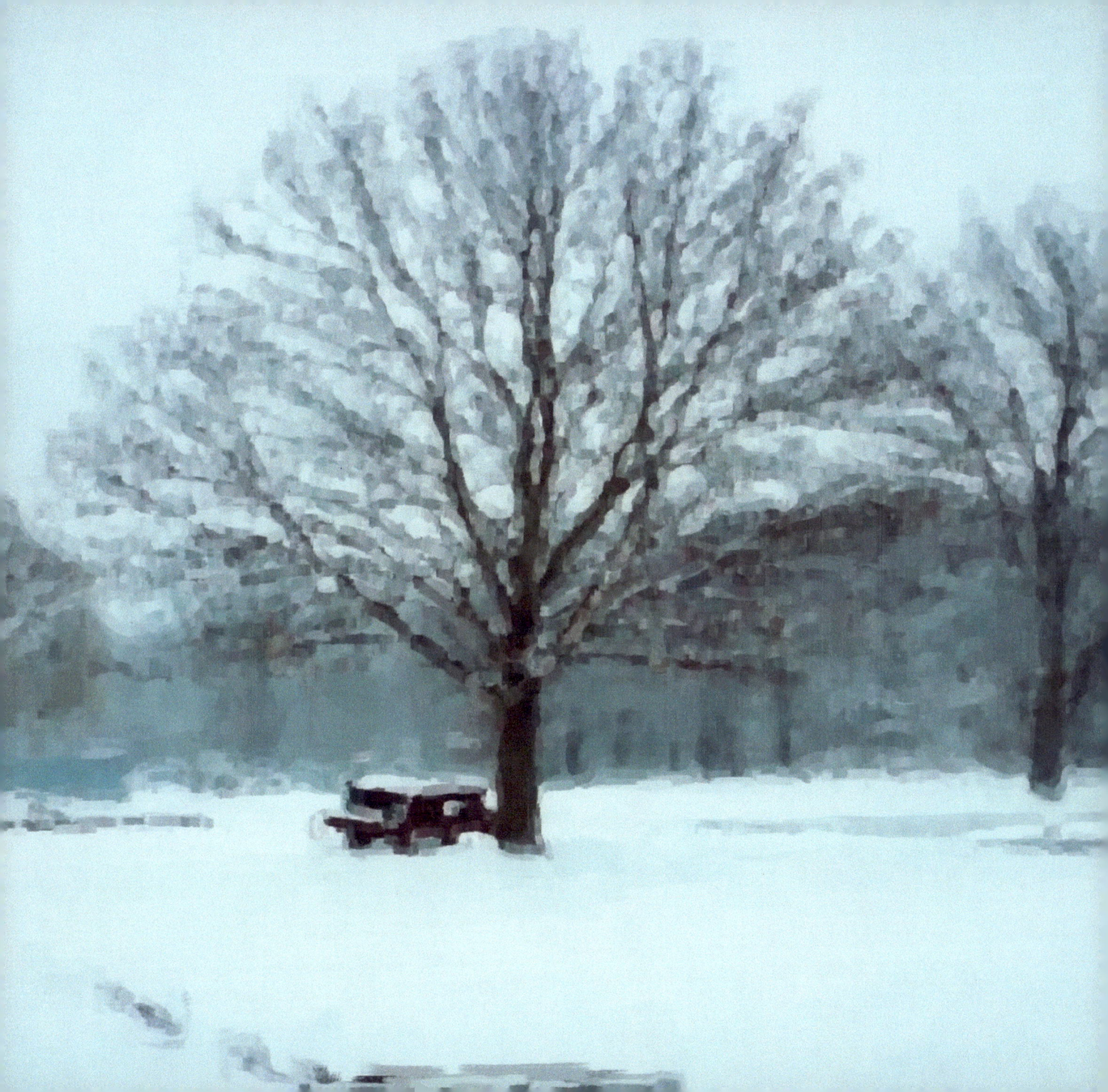

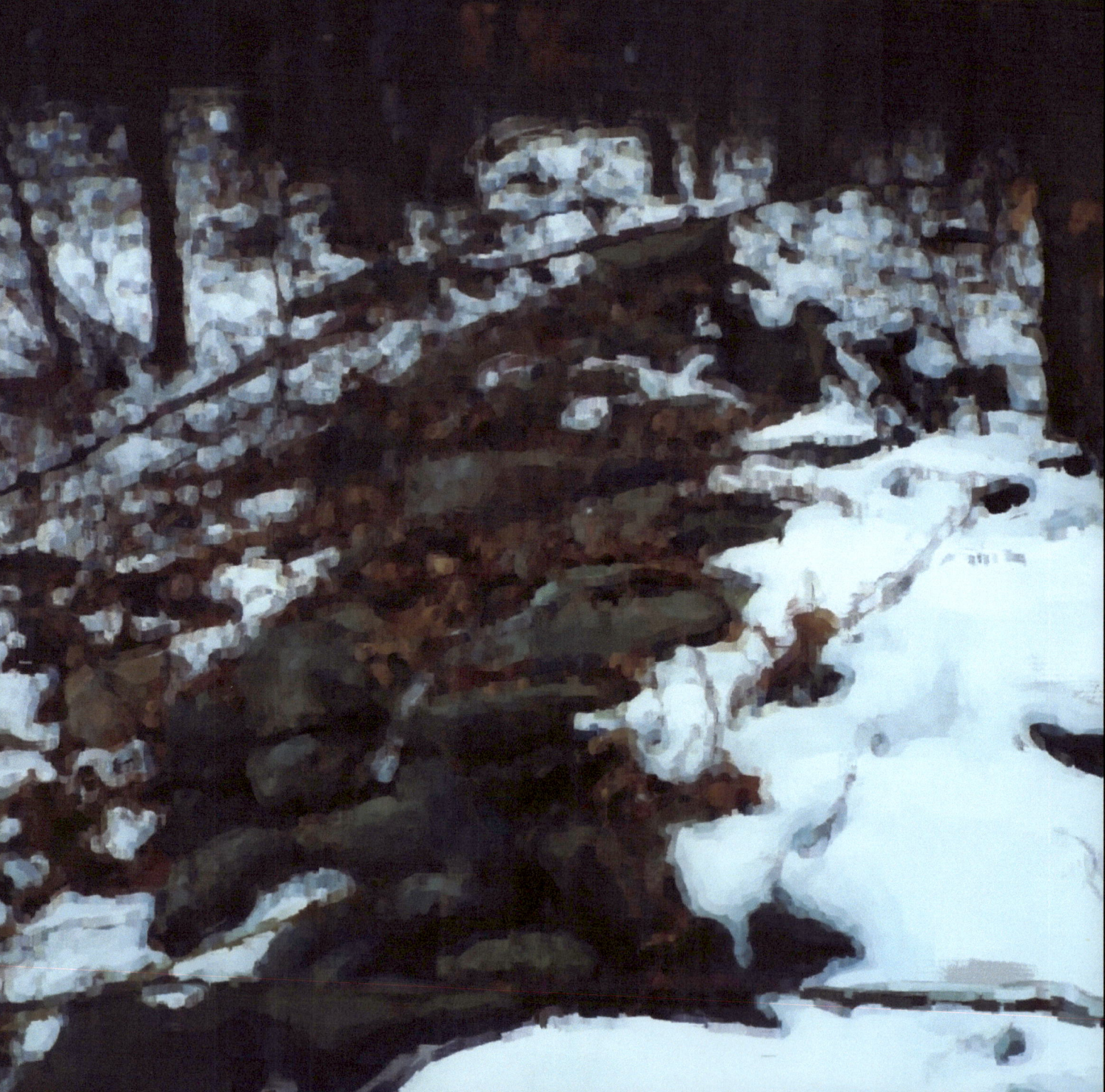

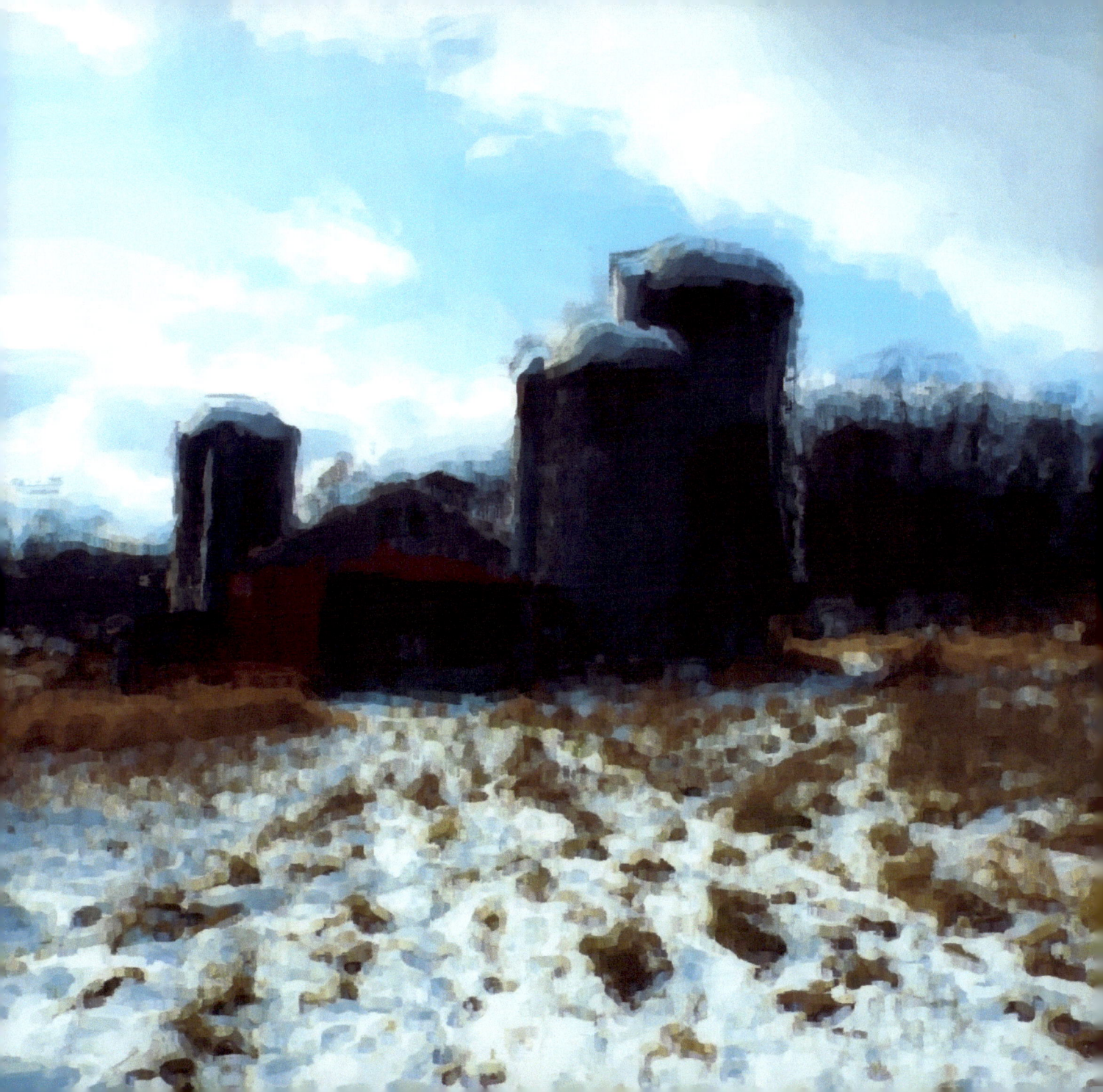

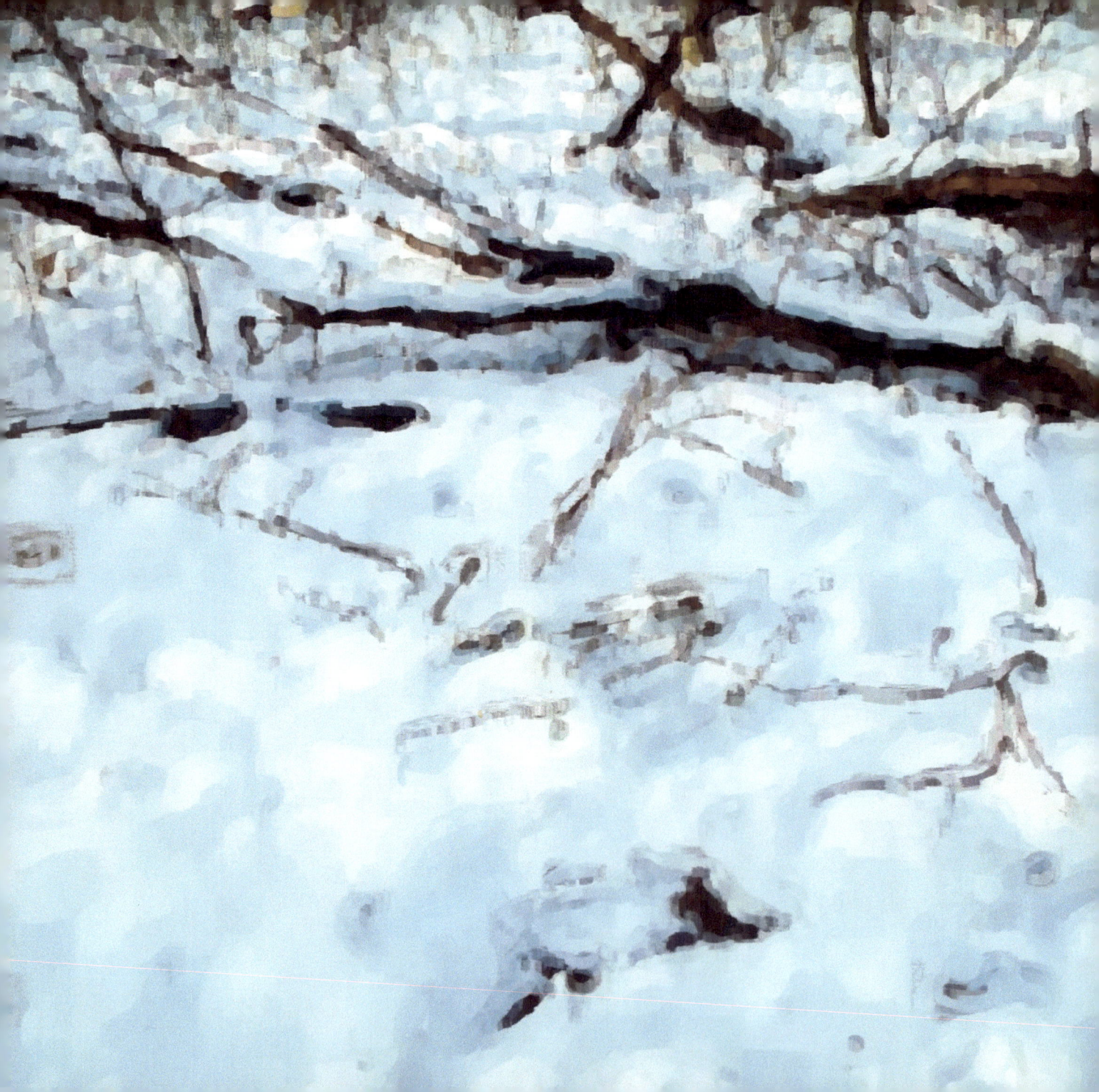

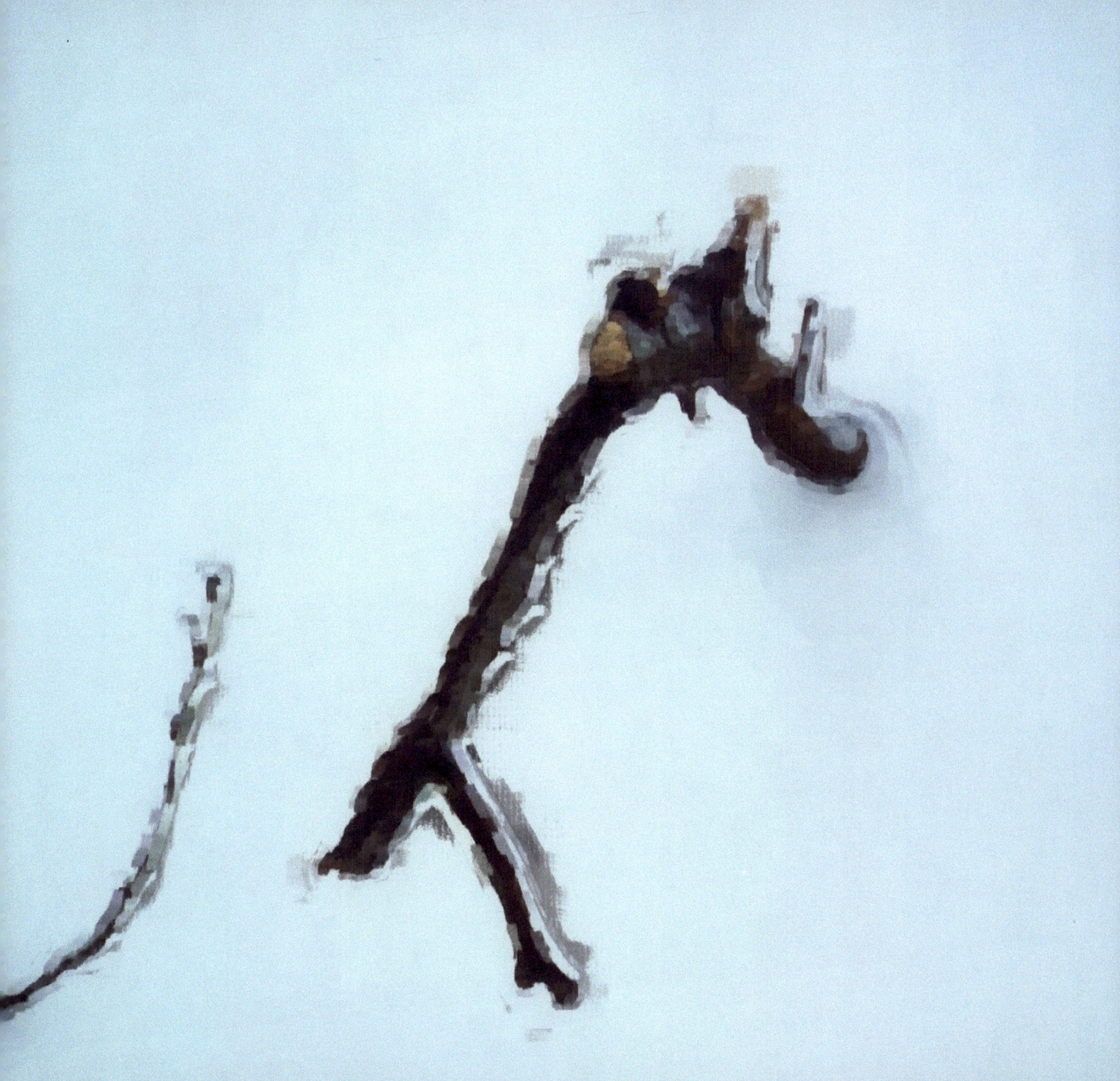

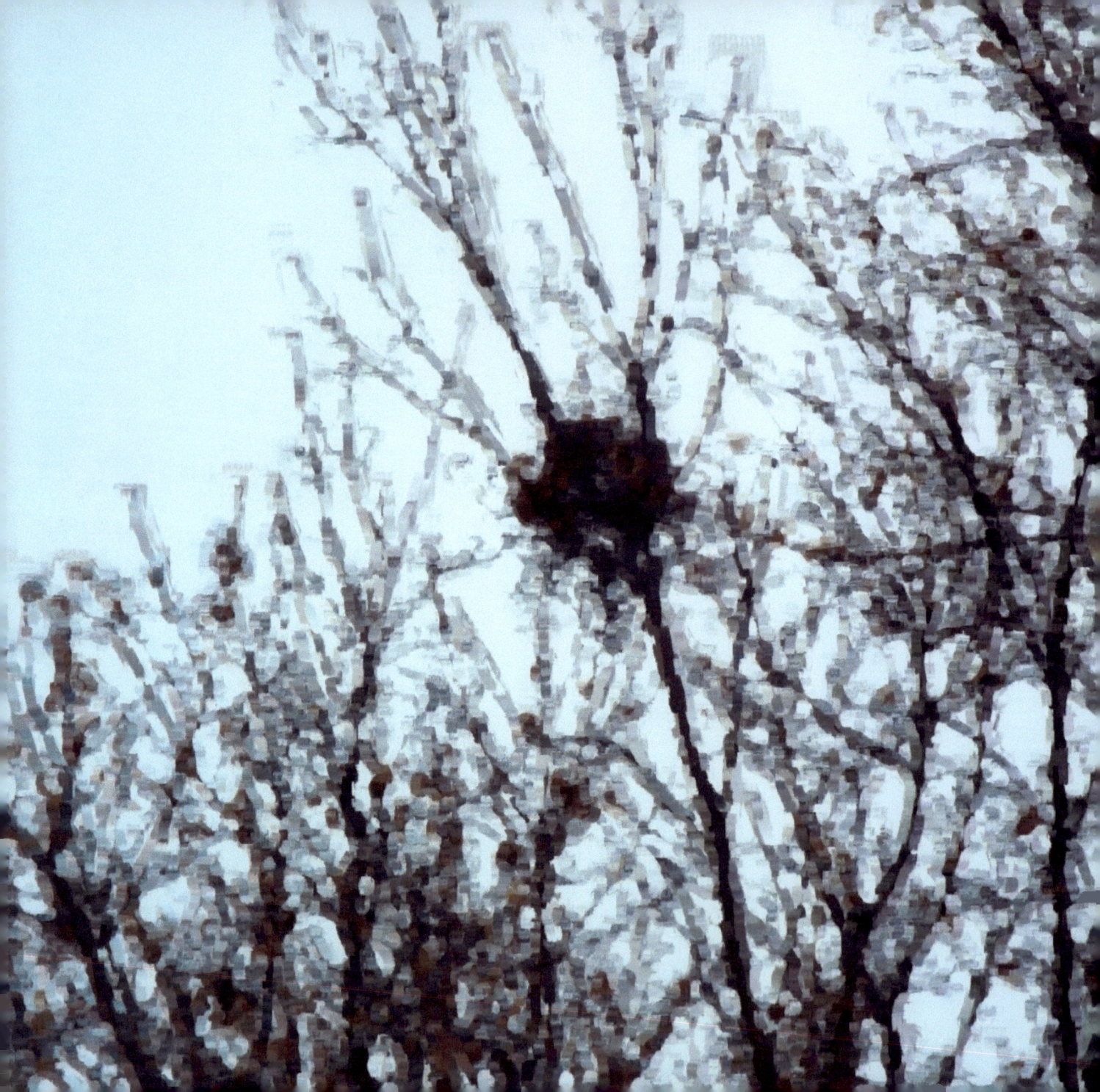

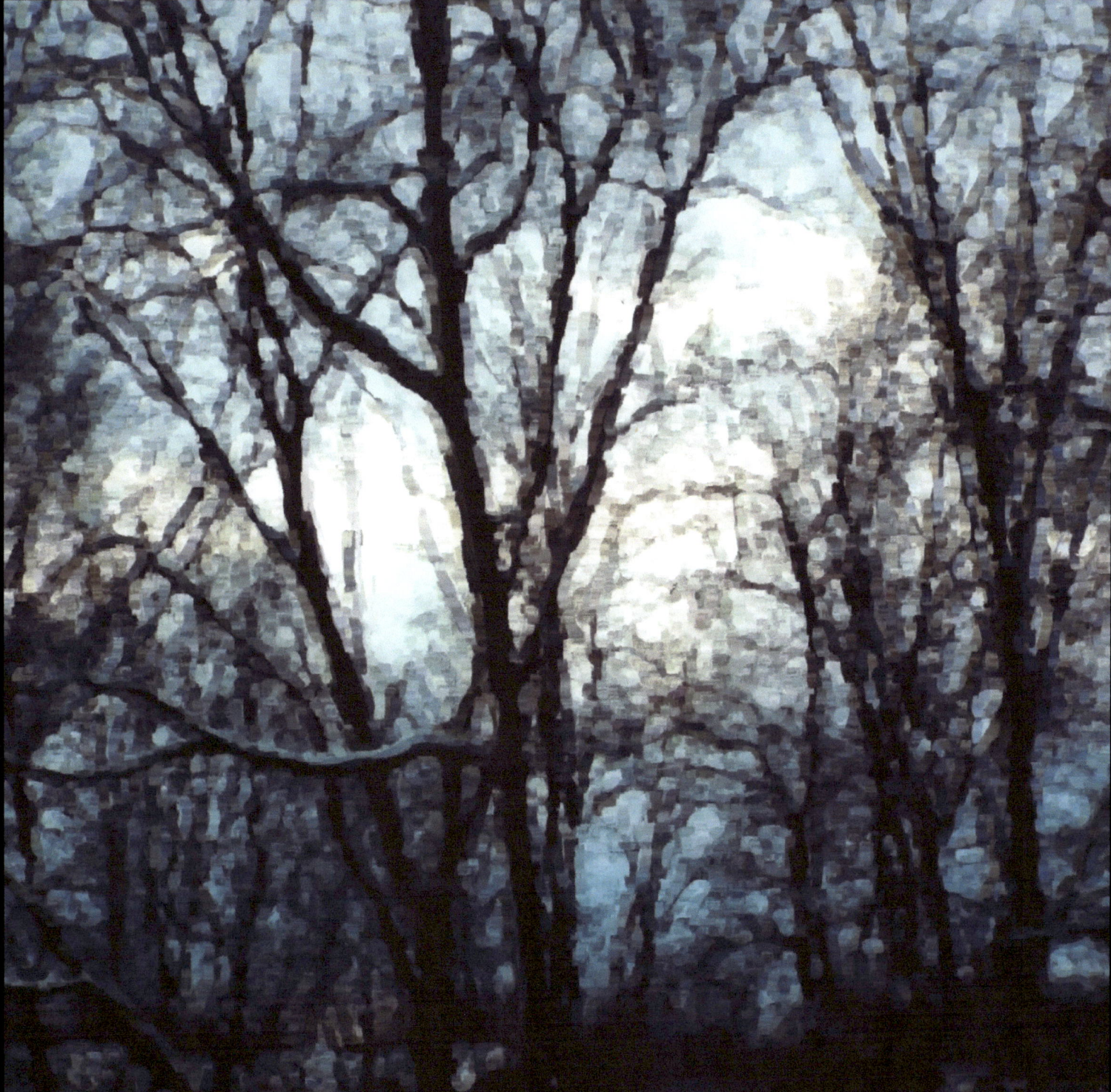

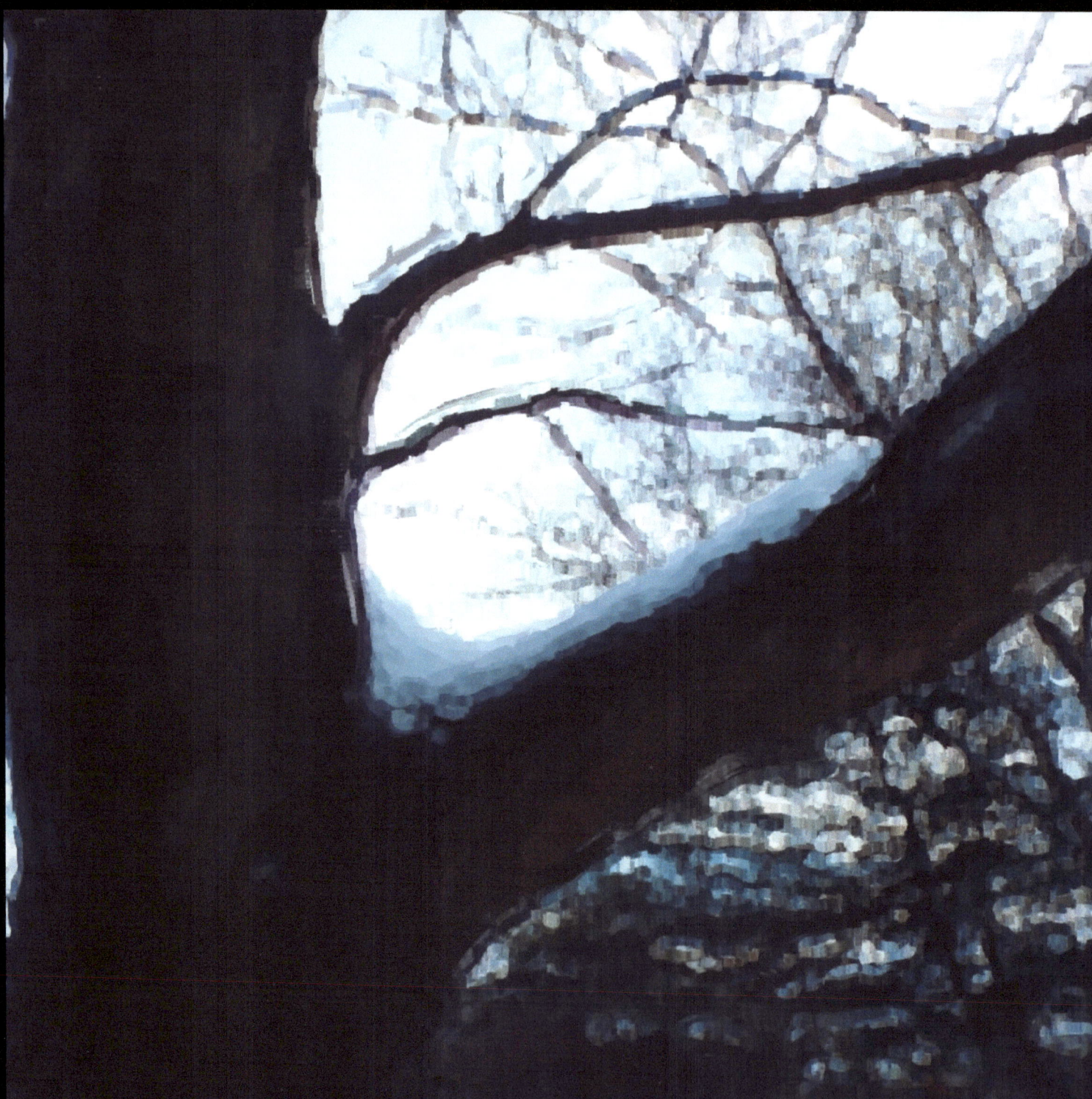

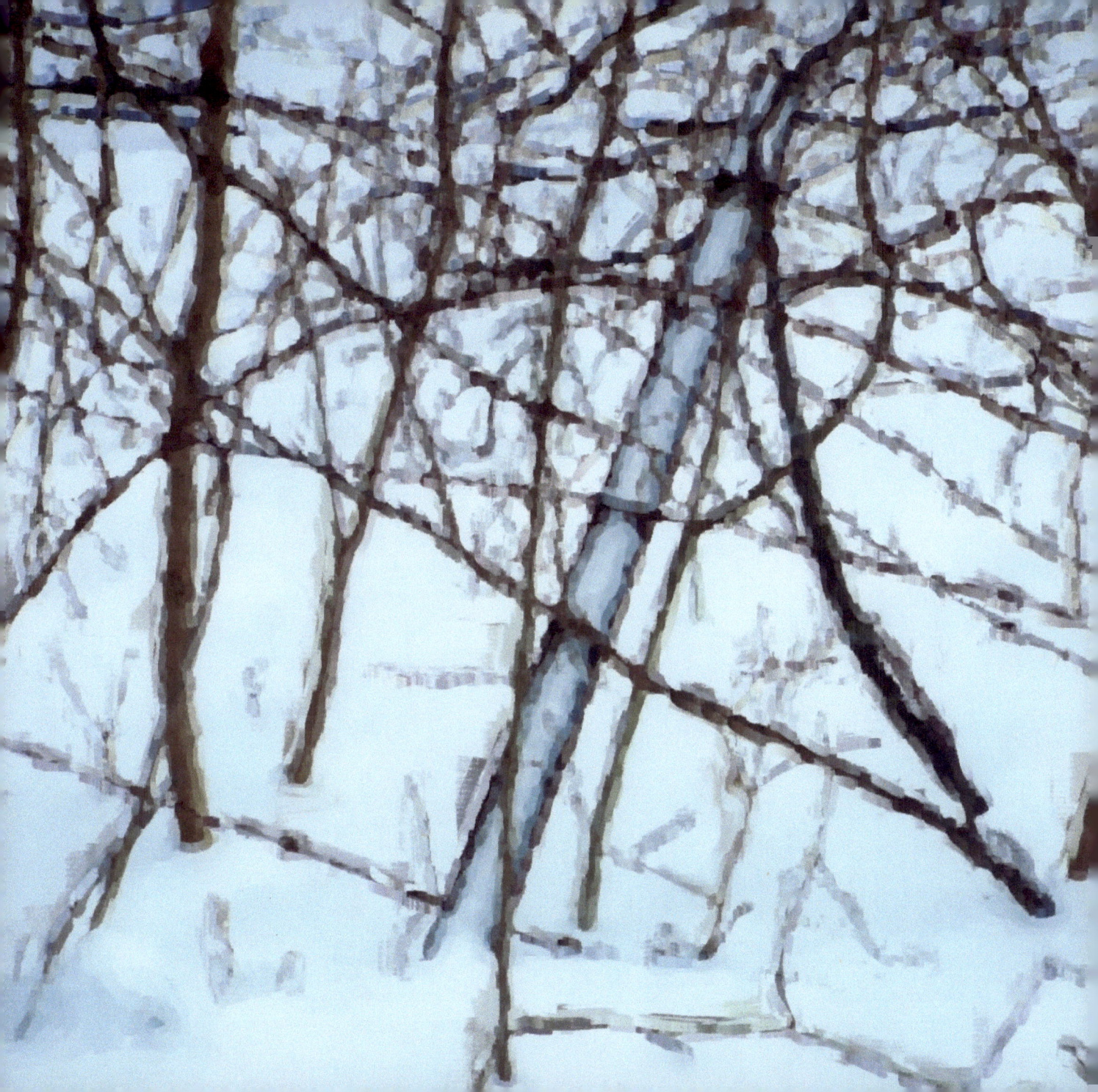

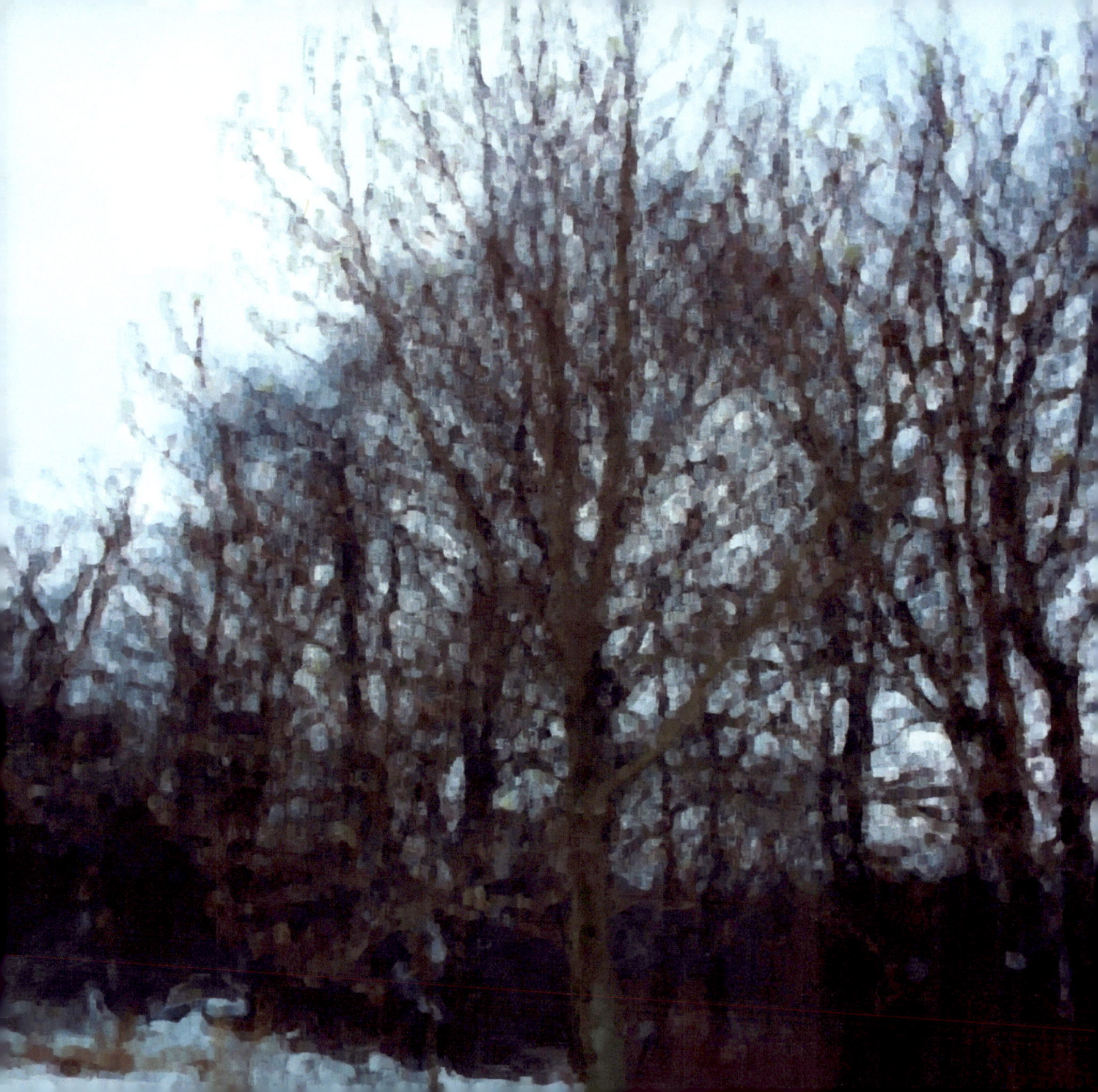

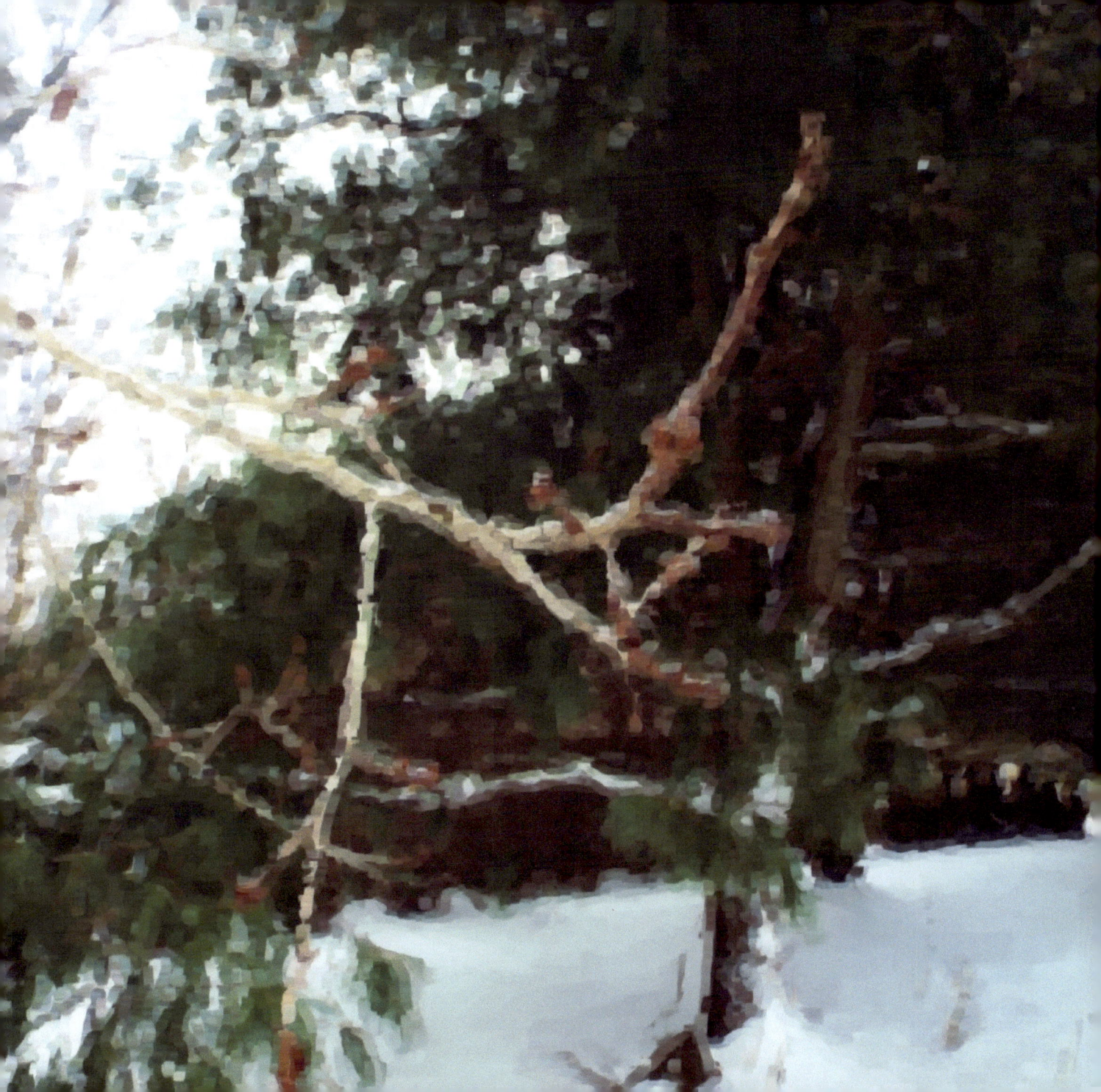

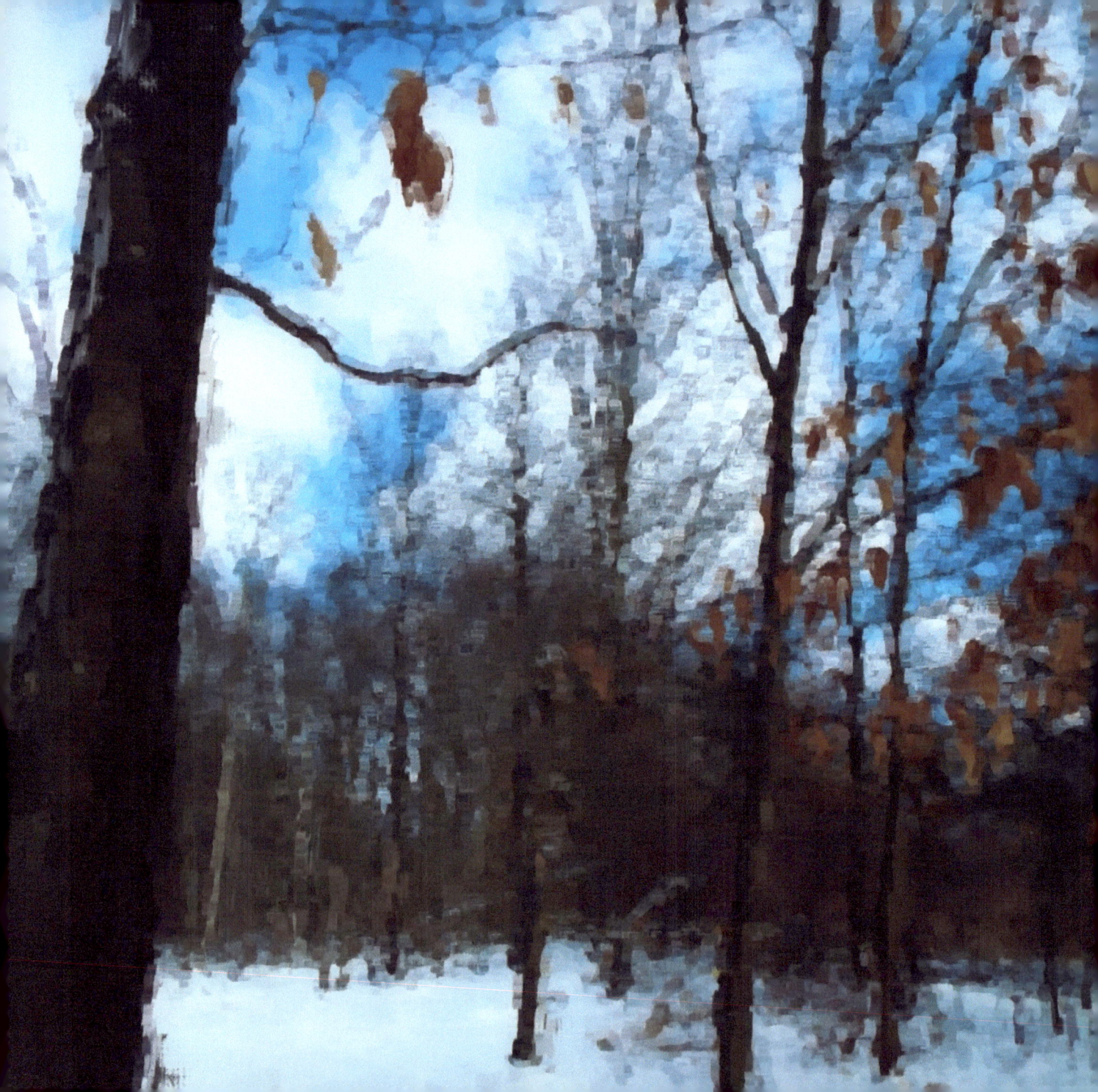

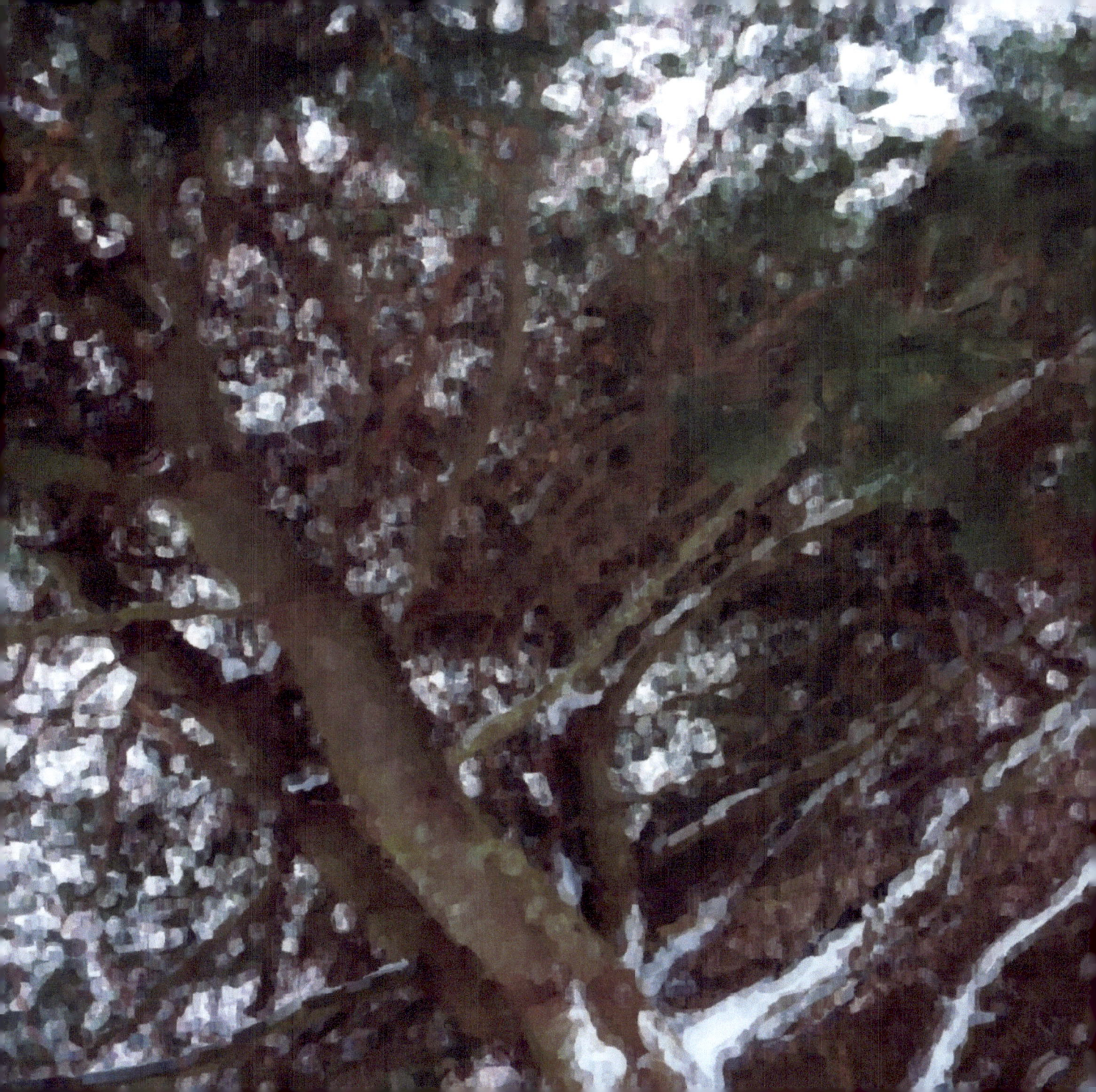

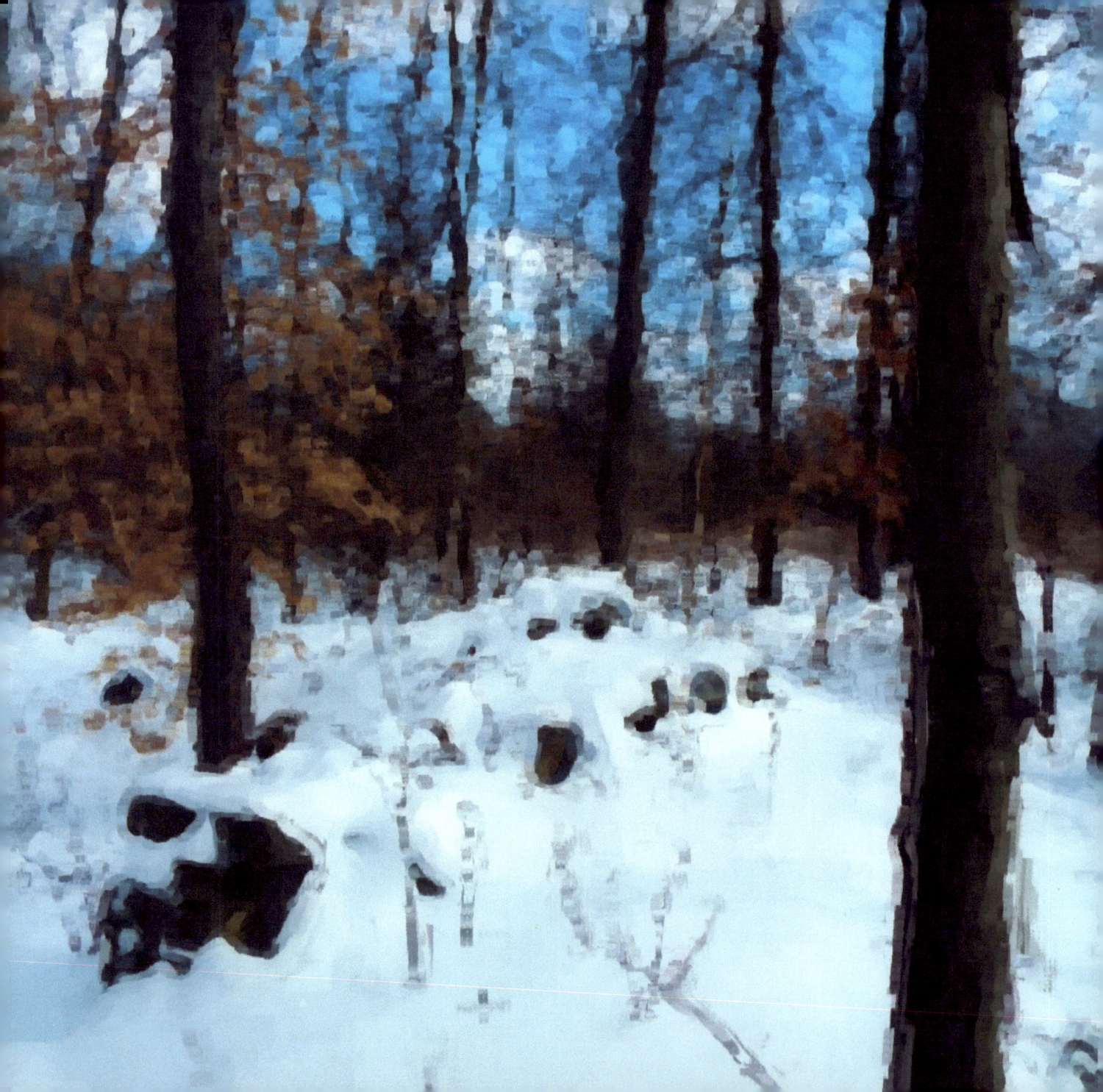

www.ingramcontent.com/pod-product-compliance
Lightning Source LLC
Chambersburg PA
CBHW040419220526
45473CB00004B/1284